I Really Meant to Tell You . . .

I Really Meant to Tell You . . .

Finding the Courage for Kindness

Jeff Hutsell

*BOOK*LOGIX®
Alpharetta, GA

ISBN: 978-1-63183-310-6

Library of Congress Control Number: 2018907994

Printed in the United States of America   0 7 0 9 1 8

☉This paper meets the requirements of ANSI/NISO Z39.48-1992 (Permanence of Paper)

Cover art by Kelli Doubek

This book is dedicated to three distinct groups of people who are all very special to me: my loving family, friends, and colleagues. Without them, this book would have become a future regret of mine with the working title of *I Really Meant to Write It . . .!*

*"I don't regret the things I have done.
I just regret the things I didn't do
when I had a chance . . ."*

—Anonymous

Contents

Acknowledgments

I would like to thank some very special people who helped me with this, my first book. To my daughter, Jennifer Scheer, for her superb "English teacher" first edit and her undying support and encouragement. To my friend and long-time associate Kelli Doubek, whose creative flair in both editorial and design helped me to really say what I wanted to say.

My eternal thanks go out to my entire family, especially my grandchildren (who have become the inspiration for EVERYTHING good in my life). Also, my friends and colleagues who selflessly contributed their personal stories and provided the true value of this book.

And thanks to the members—past, present, and future—of the Vistage Peer Advisory Boards that I have had the honor to chair. These are private groups of CEOs, business owners, and executives who help to make each other better leaders and better people. Because of your belief in me and the accountability you furnished, I could complete this part of my journey.

And finally to my team at BookLogix. These wonderful professionals helped this rookie find his way to the fulfillment of a life-long dream: to write and publish a book. They have brought this dream to many, and I, for one, say thank you for helping us all!

So, in keeping with my book title, I really want to tell you ALL that I appreciate the friendship, love, and experiences you have shared with me as I have slid down life's banister. While sometimes we picked up a few splinters along the way, you have kept me sliding smoothly down this journey we call life!

Almost My Best Speech

It was a crisp, clear fall day and it was a packed house! Family, neighbors, and friends were all in attendance and looking at me with great expectation as I stepped up to the podium. I had never been so nervous in my life, and I had given hundreds of speeches before. This one was about a very special person in my life, and I wanted to get it just right.

And I did! The classic "he knew more people than the Pope" story got them laughing, and the "he never met a stranger" got them all nodding in agreement. The retelling of his favorite joke ("My wife is SO neat that when I wake up in the middle of the night to answer nature's call, I come back in and the bed is already made!") went off without a hitch and brought the house down.

But it was when I reminisced about his life of "tilting at windmills," his constant search for improvement, and his brave and selfless service to our nation that we all agreed that this was indeed a special person.

I had accomplished what I set out to do: I paid tribute to a man I had loved and respected all my life. It was the best speech of my life, except for two rather significant details:

This tribute to my Dad was never heard by him.
This was my eulogy to him at his funeral.

"I REALLY meant to tell him . . ."

This book is my tribute to Harry Hutsell (1924–2014). There will never be another like him!

Introduction

As you may have guessed by now, the first story was my own. It is about my own regret I still have because I saved the best words I've ever said about my father until I gave his eulogy. This got me thinking about the topic of "holding back" in a broader way. The more I thought about it, the more I realized there were many things I *intend* to say to those important to me. But, alas, I haven't. Why not? Of all the things I might consider holding back (i.e. jumping from a parachute, exercising as much as I should, eating well, etc.), giving compliments seems like it would never be something to choose. It seemed a notion worthy of additional thought and study.

As I scan the social horizon today, there is a plethora of guidance and models for assertiveness training, balanced scorecards, good news/bad news stories, how to make the best deal, and more. However, there is a distinct paucity of material, models, and guidance on how to *express unconditional encouragement and love*. I mean to give it willingly, without expectation, bravely, and selflessly. I mean the kind of love that we give to puppies, kittens, and babies. The kind that for some reason isn't as easy to give to others in your life. The inevitable result of this is that not enough good news is being shared at a time when we could use it most.

As I began to write this book in the fall of 2017, it became apparent that now is the right time to discuss this topic. We find ourselves in an historically divisive era. As I think about the protests, the internet trolling, the bullying, the name calling, and the anonymous world of social media and its accompanying devices, I worry that MANY of us will regret the chances we will miss to truly connect. We will miss the chances we have to say something meaningful to those who matter to us.

It is my hope that this book will help us recognize the void, agree with the need, and find a way to change this trajectory. As Dickens's immortal character Ebenezer Scrooge said when in the presence of the Spirit of Christmas Yet to Come: "Are these the shadows of things that must be, or are they the shadows of things that MIGHT be?"

The truth is, things *can* be changed, and more often than not, it is not too late. I believe in this premise and what I strive to persuade the readers of this book. But the genesis comes from the following:

Following a thirty-five-plus year career in many areas of business leadership in public and private space, and large and small companies—including my own—I learned a lot about how to run a business, but spent as little time as possible on the "soft" side (i.e. people) of the business. In 2011, I began an unexpectedly lifechanging career as a Vistage chair. Essentially, I am responsible for facilitating several groups of executive peer advisory boards. These exist for the sole and noble purpose of helping the members become better leaders and better people. No one in the group is a competitor of another member. No one in the group is a significant customer or vendor of another member. These groups provide a safe space to share, help, problem solve, and sometimes just be an ear for each other.

That part-time avocation quickly became a full-time vocation, as I found that there is so much more than "business" if the goal is to become a better leader and better person. And after working with well over one hundred CEOs, business owners, and executives in more than five-thousand hours of one-on-one private coaching sessions, I have made a few discoveries.

This book grew from a recurring theme that, quite frankly, broke my heart every time I heard it.

I would come into the office of my client only to find them looking a bit shell-shocked and glum, and they'd say something to the effect of "You won't believe this—my star employee walked in this morning and just resigned. The one that I told you was my heir apparent, whom I loved like my own child and the one whose continued growth would allow me to finally enjoy *my* life a bit more!" This was normally followed by something like, "But, when he told me the opportunity he was given, the offer and the financial rewards, I totally understood and wished him well."

Wow! Did I hear that right?

I found this so amazing because it had happened to me in business—more than once—and with the same "rationalization" that somehow made it okay. But now, as their coach, I felt it important to dive deeper and see what we could learn. And as it turned out, almost EVERY time, when pressed, the client admitted that maybe they "assumed" they had shared all their special thoughts about being the star employee and successor with their prized associate. In fact, one of my clients even inadvertently provided me the title of this book when he told me what he said to his departing associate just before they left the office: "I REALLY meant to tell you . . ."

I swore that I would try to do something that helps make this happen less often, so I announced to my friends, family, and clients that THIS would be the topic of the book. How to avoid losing VALUED associates at work by being open, being real, being honest, and telling them how awesome they are!

When I shared that germ of an idea, universally people said, "Why stop there?" This is NOT just a business issue, this is a PEOPLE and RELATIONSHIP ISSUE. It runs the gamut from valued associate, to friends, to loved ones, to family, to old, to new, and most any relationship that exists.

So, that is how I came to write this book. In the pages to follow, I will draw on the incredible stories that were shared with me by others to illustrate many of the types and the magnitude of missed opportunities, or successful, life-changing communications that they have experienced. Each is a story that illustrates what happens when:

- We *don't* tell those we value how we really feel
- We *do* tell those we value how we really feel
- *Others tell us* how they really feel about us

I will explore why it is so challenging to do something so seemingly simple as giving GREAT news to someone we care about. Finally, we will identify specific ideas on how to overcome those challenges that have worked for others and will work for those of us willing to try them. My hope is that you will walk away with three things:

1. A recognition and acceptance of the challenges and opportunities that exist in your own relationships
2. A certainty that "words matter" and that you can do better with your communication skills if you want to
3. A series of exercises, activities, traditions, and events that others have successfully tried that have helped them overcome the inherent fear and anxiety we face when trying to have the conversations

In other words, I will show you how to find the "courage for kindness" that fuels all successful relationships.

Chapter 1
Words Matter!

Recently, the phrase "Words matter!" has been popping up all over the media, and usually in the context of someone disagreeing with what someone else has said. This book will focus on the positive way in which words can matter. It is in the conversations of our lives that so much of who we become is created. Noted author and fellow Vistage chair Susan Scott says the following:

> *"Our work, our relationships, and our lives succeed or fail one conversation at a time. While no single conversation is guaranteed to transform a company, a relationship, or a life, any single conversation can. Speak and listen as if this is the most important conversation you will ever have with this person. It could be. Participate as if it matters. It does."*
>
> — Susan Scott
> Author, *Fierce Conversations:*
> *Achieving Success at Work & in Life One*
> *Conversation at a Time*

However, the premise of *this* book is that, while I agree that so much of what we do comes from one conversation at a time, there is even more that comes from *not* having that one conversation. We are going to study many examples of where words do matter, either in their presence OR their absence. We are going to study that they matter to BOTH the givers and receivers of the words.

A friend of mine recently shared this learning with me: "The effect of someone's words is in direct proportion to their level of love and/or respect for the person speaking, AND their position of authority and/or commitment over you and/or the subject." In thinking more about this statement, I became more convinced that this statement is so true after parsing the words and coming up with these examples. Each of them is an example of how this learning applies to those in our lives.

1. **Someone for whom you have *great love and respect* but who has *no direct authority or commitment* to you.**

    An example of this is my mom, God love her. A typical quote would go something like, "My son is the world's greatest businessman!"

    Clearly, I love and respect my mom about as much as anyone on this planet. However, at age ninety, she currently has little direct authority and — at any age — was never in a position of authority to be able to state who is, in fact, "the world's greatest businessman!"

    I am flattered and dearly love her for this sentiment, BUT the effect of this statement on my life (especially as that of a businessman) is limited.

2. **Someone for whom you have *little love or respect* but who has *authority or commitment* to you or the subject.**

    An example of this might be the "boss from hell." A typical quote would go something like this: "You are my favorite employee!"

    Now, this one is a bit trickier. It is always nice to hear positive remarks from someone in authority. However, the amount of love and/or respect that you have for the speaker is a significant factor in the impact of this statement.

    Since you hold the boss in such low esteem, the best a rather hollow compliment like this can provide is a modicum of job security until you can escape from his influence. But, in fact, it probably comes across as insincere, false, or downright insulting! So, the effect on your life is also limited.

3. **Someone whom you** *love and/or respect* **a great deal AND holds** *significant authority and commitment* **to you and to the subject.**

    An example of this is might be a revered teacher from high school. A typical quote would go something like this: "You have the potential to go anywhere you want, do anything you put your mind to, and succeed beyond your wildest dreams. I am so proud of you!"

    Now, this one MATTERS. This figure of authority, who knows much more than you do about the subject matter, seems certain that you can do whatever you wish. You have always respected this teacher, and they have never given you any cause to doubt them. You are likely to hear this as sincere and honest. Also, you are most likely to believe it is true, and undoubtedly it will make a lifelong impression.

So, it is not just the compliment or "nice thing" that matters. It greatly matters WHO gave the compliment.

In addition to examining the impact of words that were shared, I would like to also spend a moment on the consequences of the same three parties NOT sharing their thoughts and sentiments with you.

Mom

- If Mom is unable to share anything that validates or confirms her love and respect for you, the areas where she holds great credibility, that is a very painful hole.
- If Mom, on the other hand, is unable to articulate her thoughts about you in areas where you do not see her as an authority, no harm, no foul.

The Boss from Hell

- If that boss is unable to articulate whether he respects you as a person or not is somewhat irrelevant, because you quite simply don't care!

- If that boss is unable to articulate how he feels about you from his status as your supervisor, that may lead to considerable angst and anxiety about job security. Even though you don't like or respect him, his opinion does matter, as it relates to your job, so it is better to have it than not.

The Revered High School Teacher

- If this special teacher never gives you any feedback about whether they like and/or respect you, this can leave a deep vacuum in your life. Whenever these voids are left in our lives, it often leads to each of us filling in the blanks. When WE fill in the blanks, they tend to be things like "I'm not enough," and that is never a good thing.
- If that teacher never gives feedback on your abilities as a student, an area where they are clearly an authority, that also leads to negative consequences. Lack of feedback is often even worse than negative feedback, because you have nothing to work with or work on.

There is a lot of potential pain when someone important to you does not share the words of love that you so desire. To illustrate this, a friend recently related a story to me about a highly impactful thing he learned about his father in a unique manner.

I Was Never Enough . . .

I guess I was about sixteen or seventeen years old and was walking through the kitchen when the phone rang. In those days, it was a real on-the-wall family phone! So, I stopped to pick it up.

The caller on the other end was a family acquaintance who worked with my dad. He identified himself, and then spent the next twenty minutes telling me what a huge mistake I was making by NOT taking advantage of my shot at the Olympics.

Just to be clear, I was in NO WAY an Olympic-caliber athlete. I was a pretty good local and state–level swimmer, but the Olympics were in no way on my radar—much less was I on theirs!

I immediately knew where this call came from, and found myself in quite a moral dilemma. A little background first: my dad was a world-class athlete who even played some baseball in the Major Leagues as a young man. I idolized him and lived all my life trying to measure up to his standards and expectations . . . whatever those were. You see, he rarely told me what his hopes and dreams were for me, but I always knew what his hopes and dreams were for himself!

I'm sure that in an effort to make himself seem amazing, my dad was the one who told his friend that his misguided son had decided unilaterally to ignore the pleadings of the Olympic Committee to participate (or something grandiose like that). That was painful for me to hear, because here I was again with the thought that I will NEVER be enough to "fit" the story my dad has in his mind about me.

So, my dilemma was what to say. Will I reject the notion, throw my dad under the bus, and expose the whole thing as a fantasy that was not true? Or, do I support my dad, take the fall, and become complicit in the lie? As you might suspect, I did the latter. I still don't know why exactly, but perhaps it is that in desiring his love so much, I was willing to do almost anything—even live a lie—if that is what I believed he wants of me.

Again, as I mentioned, I really do not know what he expected of me, but the absence of that knowledge forced me

> *to fill in the blanks. His expectation of me, at least in my*
> *mind, was and always will be MORE than I can give.*

So, from the above example, it's clear that we need ask ourselves several important questions about our relationships and our communication with the people we care about.

1. Do I know where I stand in the areas of *love* and *respect* with the people with whom I am attempting to create important connections (family, friends, work colleagues, etc.)? Do not assume you know where you stand with them or that they know where they stand with you.
2. Do I know where I stand in the areas of *authority* and *commitment* in the eyes of those with whom I am attempting to create important connections? Do not assume that because YOU see yourself as an authority that they necessarily do.

If you have taken the time and effort to understand your audience in this way, then you know the extent to which *your* words matter. Not only how much and in what ways your words matter, but you should also begin to think about how much the *absence* of your words matter as well. As noted writer Mitch Albom writes in his book *The First Phone Call from Heaven*:

"The words people do not speak are louder than the ones they do."

Psychology and sociology tell us that in the absence of information, the human response is to gravitate to imagining the worst possible outcome. In other words, if you don't tell me how you feel about something, I will make an assumption, and the odds of it being correct (or pleasant) are quite small.

Have you ever heard these statements?

- "Since you never said anything, I assumed that you didn't care!"

- "Well, I'm not a mind reader!"
- "You never say that to me anymore."

By the way, it has NO relevance that perhaps you HAVE communicated the subject once, twice, or many times, because it is not about whether or not you say it; it is about whether or not it was heard—and heard correctly.

We have all been taught to be careful of the words we speak. We have all been told again and again to find something nice to say. We have all been told again and again to know that words have consequences. But, what we really need to focus on is addressing the absence of positive and transformative words that humans have thirsted for from the beginning of time.

> *"What is left unsaid . . . says it all!"*
> —Anonymous

But, exactly what *should* you say? What do those important people in your life need to hear?

We all learned the **Golden Rule** at some point in our lives: "Do unto others what you would have them do unto you." I propose a slight alteration. Let's call it the **Golden Rule of Communicating**:

> *"Say unto others what you would have them say unto you."*

Of course, it would be great if everyone who spoke to us said exactly what *we* wanted to hear. But, it seems pretty clear to me who the winner is in that exchange.

However, some time back, I heard of what I feel is an even more relevant rule.

It is an upgraded Golden Rule, called the **Platinum Rule**. I call our version the **Platinum Rule of Communicating**, which is:

Say unto others what they would have you say unto them.

Do you see the subtle difference here? It is obvious that if you wish to be understood in a foreign country, speak to them in their language, not your own. So, why is it not equally obvious that in trying to communicate to an important person in your life, that you need to speak in "their language" instead of yours? For example, which would you rather hear from your boss:

"What I like about you is that you always do everything I ask, exactly the way I tell you to, and never complain. You are a good member of my crew!"

OR

"What I admire most about you is you understand my *intent*, but you figure everything out so independently and maturely, and it makes me trust and respect you more than you can ever know. I am honored to have you on our team!"

Both approaches say similar things, but it seems to me that the second approach is MUCH more about the listener than it is about the speaker. It is my guess that the second approach is closer to the way the listener would like to be talked to. Both are compliments, but only one will really serve to inspire the listener in a meaningful way.

We have been taught that the goal of good communication is to try to get YOUR message across to others. However, if the desired outcome is to build and grow relationships, perhaps the goal should focus more on getting the message THEY wish to hear across in a way that speaks your truth and uses their language.

All too often, we are either unwilling or unable to come up with the right words. The result is a failed outcome that satisfies neither the speaker nor the listener. As the chain-gang captain said in the classic movie *Cool Hand Luke*, "What we have here is a failure to communicate."

Chapter 2
A Failure to Communicate

As a business leader, and more recently as a business coach, I have noticed again and again that the lowest scores given to companies and leaders in associate surveys fall in the area of communications. No matter the size of the company, no matter where they are, and no matter what they do, the rating for "communicates well" always is one of the lowest ratings in employee-engagement surveys.

Of course, outside of business, I have noticed the same things about marriages, families, friendships, governments, politics, etc. So many personal relationships suffer and sometimes succumb to the subject of poor or nonexistent communication by one party or the other.

At a time when there are thousands of conflicting and confusing messages coming at you 24/7, from more sources, devices, and technologies than ever before, we must ask why. Why is it that we are still unable to achieve anything close to great—or even adequate—communication?

This is just one person's opinion, but after trying to solve this riddle for nearly forty years in business and even longer in my life, I have developed a hypothesis for you to consider, the ONLY two things most people really need to take away from communications with those they respect and care about.

Let's call them our **Fundamental Questions**:

I realize that one could read the above two questions in a way to see only cynicism and self-absorption. However, I believe that the above two questions relate very closely to a theory we all learned in Psychology/Sociology 101. Below, you will find the familiar Maslow's Hierarchy of Needs pyramid. I believe that these **Fundamental Questions** relate to nearly all of these human needs.

Maslow's Hierarchy of Needs

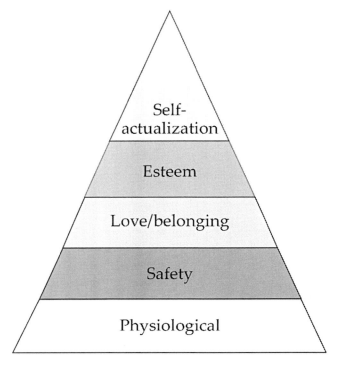

1. **The basic physiological needs**

    We all have the need to be healthy and have our basic needs provided.

    How does this relate to our **Fundamental Questions?** Not knowing how others view us creates anxiety, sleeplessness, and worry, depriving us of some of our physiological needs and, ultimately, affecting our health.

2. **The need to be safe and secure**

    We all have the need to enjoy the safety and security of a home, enough money, a job, and a family.

    How does this relate to our **Fundamental Questions?** Not knowing where we stand with others and what that might mean for us is neither a safe nor a secure feeling.

3. **The need to be loved and to belong**

    We all have the need to be a part of something bigger than ourselves.

    How does this relate to our **Fundamental Questions?** Not knowing how or if you fit in with others is a huge risk to achieving this feeling of belonging and being loved.

4. **The need for self-esteem**

    We all need confidence, respect, and achievement.

    How does this relate to our **Fundamental Questions?** If we do not get the feedback we need to feel like we are worthy, have succeeded, or deserve reward, our self-esteem is significantly reduced.

5. **The need for self-actualization**

    We all want to experience meaning and purpose in our life, as well as acceptance, morality, and creativity.

    How does this relate to our **Fundamental Questions?** A lot of our ability to self-actualize comes from experiencing the positive feedback and affirmation of others to know we have a purpose that means something to more than ourselves. Never receiving this input from those who are meaningful to us becomes a barrier to achieving this all-important goal.

So, why is it, then, that we fail to communicate such simple things? Why are so many of us making the following complaints nearly every day?

- "This company never communicates anything."
- "My spouse never communicates with me."
- "My sibling/friend/coworker/etc. is the worst at communication."

What we, the ever-rational communicators, hear is that we need to communicate MORE!

- More often
- More clearly
- More media
- More messages
- More repetition
- More blogging, posting, emailing, calling, talking
- . . . More . . . more . . . of everything!

What we should be hearing is:

"I am *not* communicating what they want (need) to hear. Therefore, if they don't hear that, they are not going to hear anything!"

Marshall McLuhan, the great sixties guru of media and communication, may have been wrong when he said, "The medium is the message." In fact, it is the message that people are ravenously seeking and often not finding in the cacophony of media.

In addition to sending the wrong message, we also know that the failure to communicate can come in at least two other very common ways. One is to purposely choose *not* to communicate at all. For this, the speaker must ultimately bear the responsibility. The other is to communicate in such a way the listener does not receive the message you intended to send. This responsibility also falls on the speaker and is even more of a sad situation because we may not even understand what has happened.

The net result is often a material change in the relationship and a significant regret for both parties. Examples of painful relational regrets are:

- *Resignation of a valued associate*
  The chosen one, the one you were counting on for your future. You promoted them, gave them raises and public praises, and yet they left. What happened?

- *Fading of a friendship that you always counted on*
  We were inseparable. We used to finish each other's sentences. Years could go by and we could pick it up just where we left it . . . until we couldn't. What happened?

- *The end of a romantic relationship*
  They said it was 'til death do us part, or a love that would never die, or "You guys are the perfect couple." Of course my partner knew how I felt. How could they not? I did everything for them. What happened?

- *Loss of a family member*
  In the lifetime of a relationship lived one day, one year, one decade after the other, of course they knew how I felt. Or did they? A very common regret is expressed as "I just wish I had one more day or one more conversation." What happened?

Nothing happened—that's the problem. There are a million logical explanations but very few good reasons. However, the regret is real, and sometimes lasts forever. When we think about it, we all know that. We know that every relationship needs care, feeding, love, and nurturing, and never can be taken for granted. We know that when we do NOT speak our love, the relationship will suffer, fade, and perhaps end.

Regret like that is what we disclose on our deathbeds. The "I wish I had" speech is usually about family, friends, and relationships. But, for some reason, we often fail in the care and feeding of this MOST important thing we cherish. Why?

Chapter 3
Why Is Good News So Hard to Give?

The solution should be quite simple, right? Just tell people how you feel about them honestly, directly, and in exactly the way they wish to hear it. So, why do we fail to do that so often? Why is it so difficult?

I believe there are several reasons all encapsulated by two main categories: Society and Our Own Fears.

Society

Society and our American culture say that we *must* have continuous improvement. Stop for a moment to say "Good work," and then move onwards and upwards. All compliments need to be offset with ways to improve. It seems we read more "self-improvement" books than any other genre. What is there to congratulate when we think there is so much left to do and so far to go? So, most of the time we just don't do it. We do not stop to take the time to remind others of where they stand in the **Fundamental Questions**. So, while the quest for improvement and constant growth is fine, it is not possible without the fundamental issues of "how am I doing with you" and "what does that mean for me" being completely communicated and received.

One of my pet peeves is the "balanced compliment." You know the one; it goes something like this, "You did an amazing job on that last project. It was done on time, under budget and the customer loved it, BUT . . ."

Studies have shown that whenever a sentence is interrupted by the word BUT, everything prior to the word is immediately discounted or forgotten and ONLY the part that follows is assumed to be true. What a waste! We spend all that time working on a nice compliment and don't even know that we have sabotaged it with the "balancing BUT" inserted into the middle.

Try to imagine hugging your little baby and saying, "Daddy loves you BUT . . ." or how about if the traditional wedding vows looked like this "to have and to hold, from this day forward, for better, for worse, for richer, for poorer, in sickness and in health, until death do us part, BUT . . ." Ridiculous right? However, it really is no different than the "constructive and balanced compliments" we give to those around us.

Job performance reviews are perhaps the most noted offender of this. For something that is a part of nearly every company's culture and tradition, it is amazing to me how poorly these are viewed. They are equally dreaded by both the giver and the receiver.

Why? Because there is an expectation of a "balanced scorecard" where we *must* come up with the good *and* the bad. Why? And in most cases, both sides of the review are a complete surprise to the receiver. If we had a relationship of value with each other we would already know how we both feel, and not have to wait around for some arbitrary form, format, and date to find out.

Our Own Fears

While it is easy to blame society, the HR department, the boss, etc. for this "lack-of-communication issue," a significant part of that problem lies in our own fears and insecurities. And remember, I am not saying that these are logical or rational fears or insecurities, but ones that just *are*.

For example, someone might worry, "What if I say the compliment the wrong way and look foolish?" Wow! So, let me get this straight. Your intention is to go to someone with whom you already have an established relationship built on trust, and tell them how incredibly wonderful they are and how they bring sunlight and rainbows into your world . . . and the fear is that they will reject this out of hand due to poor wording? Really?

"When is the right time?" This one is really a challenge. In a great long-term relationship, we struggle to find the "perfect time" to tell the other person how we feel. It is kind of awkward to say, "Oh, by the way . . . you rock my world," out of the blue. We wish there was a time and a place where it was safe to say these things. At least, that is what we tell ourselves.

How many of us have asked someone to lunch, to go on a walk, etc. with the sole intent of telling them exactly how we feel about them and their absolute value to us? We make the arrangements, think about what we will say, head for the venue, make small talk in the car. After an hour or so, we find ourselves back in the car heading back to work, thinking, *Well, maybe next time. The opportunity really didn't present itself,* or *It didn't feel right.* I have done this many times in many different relationships and situations, and that excuse still seems like the weakest of all. It sounds more like fear presented itself and opportunity never had a chance.

Why does this happen?

- *We really have no idea what to say.*
  This is much more common than you might realize. Because we have little practice in highly effective compliments (or communicating in general, for that matter), we are often at a loss of what words to use at all. How many times has our inability to find the words caused us to say nothing at all? We are so worried about finding the perfect words, we resort to the ultimate imperfection: silence.

- *What if it goes to their head?*
  This is often a worry when you are responsible for the person being complimented, such as a direct-reporting work associate or a young child. Somewhere along the way, we have been told that compliments are somehow taken by those who receive them as a weapon to be used to "lord it over" others and feel superior.

- *Do we even want to?*
  Jealousy and envy are still significant elements of the

human psyche. Sometimes paying a compliment is difficult because we often are complimenting them on something we are lacking. For example, one might want to say, "You are the most amazing and outgoing person. Whenever you enter a room, you fill it with your presence in a positive and uplifting way!" Obviously, that would even make the most outgoing extrovert blush. However, wonderful expressions like this are often withheld because of the envy felt by the person who was thinking about saying it.

Can we ever get over our true insecurities about this type of talk? *True* sharing of feelings involves one-on-one, eyeball-to-eyeball, real discussions. Not group hugs, not emails, not "likes," but real exchange! Nothing creates insecurity like deciding to walk up to someone and tell them exactly how you feel. It is much easier to talk *about* them than *to* them.

A friend has the following to say about sharing. It resonates very well in a society that is now about validation measured by the quantity of views, "likes," thumbs up, smiley faces, and even piles of poop emojis that they receive.

If you tell five people about someone, it validates YOU. If you ONLY tell that one person, it validates THEM.

Sadly, the first statement is merely the opposite side of bullying, because a compliment behind your back is not a lot different than an insult behind your back. In both cases, the teller *mainly* cares about themselves.

The second is the stuff of bravery. It is not easy to do, there is little public acclaim, and it is solely intended to help the person receiving it. When you MUST tell someone, and silence is not an option, you just have to go for it. By doing so, you have exhibited both bravery AND love.

"In the end, we will remember not the words of our enemies, but the silence of our friends."
—Dr. Martin Luther King, Jr.

If fact, good news is always hard to give. It never gets easier, and we all need help and practice to learn how to do it. But before we even set out to do it, we need to consider our motive.

Chapter 4
What's Your Motive?

As Simon Sinek warns in his groundbreaking book *Start with Why*, people don't remember you for how you do things or what you do nearly as much as why you do it. What is your true motivation for doing whatever it is you are doing? In this case, we are referring to this question:

"WHY am I telling you this?"

I mentioned earlier that the level of your relationship relates directly to the impact of your statements to people (i.e. Mom, Boss from Hell, or Revered Teacher from Chapter 1). Just as important is your motive. We are all very adept at understanding—or at least *thinking* we understand—why someone does or doesn't say the words that they do. And we use that assumption to assess and answer our **Fundamental Questions** of "How am I doing with you?" and "What does that mean for me?"

If we don't say anything at all, then our relationship must rely upon whatever assumption the other person makes based on little or no data—and we all know how that works out. Even worse is what happens when our "other" believes that our "WHY" is based on a selfish or self-serving motive.

Here are some examples of this:

- Our other believes we are saying what we are saying to "gain" something from the relationship.
- Our other believes that we are saying what we are saying to avoid losing the relationship at an inopportune time, and looking weak or foolish.
- Our other believes we are saying what we are saying

with a complete misunderstanding of what they are truly needing to hear.

In other words, the message is lost when it is believed that the motivation is all about YOU and nothing about ME or US. This makes the effort not only wasted, but likely damaging. Put yourself in this situation and think about how this boss makes you feel:

> "I know how hard you have been working, and I thank you for it and promise to make it worth your while soon. BUT, I have to wait until the right time and need you to double down and really push to make this quarter's goals happen. Trust me, I'm going to the top and taking you with me."

If I was as exhausted and felt as taken advantage of as this person must feel, I would certainly entertain the next phone call from a recruiter, wouldn't you?

The real friend, the true companion and partner, will think before they speak. The thoughts they will have would sound something like:

> "I know how hard you have been working. It means so much to me to have someone like you on my team. Trust is the most important part of a relationship, and I want you to know that I trust you completely. It would be an honor to have you be a part of my team for as long as you wish. Together, we can do important things and have fun doing so."

You can see the answers to the two fundamental questions in *this* version. You would certainly know "how you are doing with me." Likewise, you will know "what that means to you." And there was never any mention of money, raises, time off, etc. Rather, there is an understanding of a relationship built on trust.

In this example, the boss is thinking, *I'm acutely aware of the influence I have over my team. I realize that is a lot of power. However, I choose to use that power for their good . . . not mine!* This is the sentiment of someone who has the right motivation for their words. It is all about the other person and not at all about themselves. It is about the relationship and making it stronger together, not winning or losing the moment.

From my personal memory, I can easily recall both encouraging and discouraging words from ten years ago or even longer! The words themselves might be a bit of a blur, but the result of the words sticks with me. I will never forget what my high school football coach told me during our last practice before the big game. He yelled to me and four other guys, "Come over to this side of the field and stand close together. I need someone to block the view of this play from the road." I'm not even sure those were his words, but I do remember feeling the statement as this: "Hutsell, I need someone to be a human wall, and since you aren't much of a football player, maybe you can handle that!"

> *"I've learned that people will forget what you said, people will forget what you did, but people will never forget how you made them feel."*
> —Maya Angelou

I'm sure he never even thought about what he said, but I did. It isn't just the large pronouncements or big events that affect each of our lives.

> *"Sometimes someone says something really small, but it fits right into this empty space in your heart."*
> —Unknown

Sometimes, it isn't much at all, but it certainly can be either a small, painful thing or a small, wonderful thing. Size doesn't matter; what matters most is where the comment lands!

So, even if you know why you are doing it, and it is for all the right reasons, there remains the matter of the actual event. How you say it, when you say it, where you say it are all a part of the equation for a successful communication.

Chapter 5
How Do You Do It?

"Always be kind when it is possible . . . and it is ALWAYS possible."
—Dalai Lama

Like many things in life that are "good for you," there is also a difficult challenge to saying the right thing. It is not easy; it is foreign to most of us, and the "how" and "when" often get in the way of the "what" and "why." This is one of those times where logistics can trump need, meaning, motive, or importance. In order to have effective communication, you need to prepare yourself thoroughly. This is because, as I have said before, this is hard, and for most of us, it is not natural.

First, you must allow yourself to be vulnerable. Being vulnerable means putting yourself out there, risking everything to have the chance at the positive outcome you desire. Being willing to be vulnerable means being willing to do it wrong to make it right. You might mess up, say it badly, or make a mistake, but it is worth it to keep going until it is "made right." Being brave and selfless is the key to being willing to be vulnerable. You must care more for the other person than for yourself.

Next, you just must decide that the cost is zero and the potential reward is infinite. How can you lose in this proposition? The cost is zero, because all you intend to do is tell someone how much they mean to you and how wonderful they are. These are thoughts and feelings translated into bravely delivered words. This costs nothing but the courage to deliver them. You are not trying to improve them, criticize them, persuade, or even befriend them. You are only trying to recognize and honor them in a positive way.

Now, put yourself in their shoes. Remember the **Platinum Rule**: "Say unto others as they would have you say unto them." If you were them, would you be offended or hurt by an unconditional compliment? If someone told you that you were a role model for them, or that you are the best friend they ever had, and wanted nothing in return, would you be upset? When put in these terms, it is inconceivable that we can fear the conversation, because we all would give anything for the chance to hear those nice things said to us. In fact, these are much more than "nice things;" these are the words that can be life altering. Knowing that the person you are about to speak to will be thrilled to hear positive, life-altering words said about them is the truth, and should help overcome that trepidation we all have.

Then, do not overthink it. When you come into the presence of a baby or a puppy, do you think through the strategy of how you approach them and what you say? Or, do you just jump right in with words of happiness, comfort, and unconditional love? Something happens when the object of our affection grows older and can really understand us. We immediately begin to worry about how they will react. Again, this only serves as head noise that we have to work to silence in order to communicate what we really want to communicate—and what they really want to hear!

Finally, expect to give and not to get. If you have the correct motive, then all you care about is the other person; all you want is for them to receive your intended message. It is natural to desire positive feedback. We should not expect anything in return. Not "thank you," not "I've been waiting all my life for you to say that," not "That is the most amazing thing I have ever heard," and not even "You had me at hello!" Likewise, we should not expect to hear "That was a terrible thing to say," nor "I'm really upset you told me that," nor "Your grammar is terrible, and you were stammering!"

Even if we do receive statements like those, it doesn't matter if our motive was the right one. Win or lose, we wanted to tell someone how we feel about them and how important they are to us. If they do or do not reciprocate, that is another issue, but not the reason we made the statement.

We can never really know what the receiver of our good news will do. But, even if we are rejected or if the news is not received with the enthusiasm we had hoped for, we are still miles ahead in the game. Remember, the cost of silence is dear. It is called *regret*, and that is one thing that we all want to keep from our lives.

The statement is a one-way proclamation, not the beginning of a conversation or negotiation. We don't say to our star team member, "So, if I told you that you were awesome and gave you a raise, would you guarantee that you will not take another job?" That sounds terrible, but sometimes, we actually approach someone with our kind words only when it is too late, or they have mentally moved on. It is rarely too early to give someone encouragement, and it is often too late.

Finally, as stated before, recognize that changing our trained learning of *society* and *our own fear* to follow the above advice is hard. But every time we do it, like other things, we get better at it. While it never gets easier, its importance never wanes. Like all of life's "good habits," the destination is well worth the journey!

Chapter 6
The Stories

In prior chapters, I have outlined the numerous challenges that face each of us who "really meant to tell you." Those varied and manifold reasons and explanations should validate why it is so hard to do this. There is a lot of friction involved with taking a chance and saying exactly what we want to say to someone. Also, they show us that many of us feel the same challenges. You are *not* alone!

I am struck by the number of times I've asked a CEO, upon completing their first Vistage peer advisory board meeting, what they thought about it, and how similar most of their answers are. "I was relieved to discover that I was not the only one that . . ."

The fact that we are not alone in our words or deeds is and has always been comforting.

The struggles we all feel and strive to overcome are universal. It is much easier to take them on if we are not alone, which is why our relationships are so important to us.

Therefore, I decided to devote a great deal of this book to

allowing us to have our own peer advisory board. You will spend time reading the stories of many different people in their own words from all over the country, of all ages and backgrounds. They will describe their own stories that put into practice the principles of the previous five chapters. In doing this, it is my sincere hope that you, too, will feel the relief of "I am not the only one who . . ."

More importantly, just as in all peer advisory board meetings, we will have the benefit of learning about others as they strived, failed, conquered, or benefited from these issues. While none of these are *exactly* the same as what we are facing, the similarities are striking, and I'm certain you will find great value in seeing your challenges through the lenses of others' experiences. Reflecting upon this always adds comfort and clarity, and hopefully will also give some great ideas that you can use, too!

Toward that end, I went out to over two hundred members of my network and asked them to contribute their stories. In that request, I asked the following questions.

I would like you to share a personal story about one or more of the following questions about a relationship(s) that you have had. The categories and questions are as follows:

1. Stories of Regret

Tell me about a time where you believe a relationship was significantly impacted because you didn't really tell the other person how much they meant to you.

a. *What was the nature of the relationship (business, family, romantic, friend, etc.)?*

b. *Tell me about how it ended (resigned, passed away, walked out, faded out, etc.).*

c. *Tell me what you now think you should have said.*

d. *Tell me why you did not say it (fear or rejection, no urgency, assumed they knew, etc.). Did you ever come close? What stopped you?*

2. Stories of Redemption

Tell me about an experience where you did take the time to say exactly what was on your mind and feel that action impacted the relationship.

a. *What was the nature of the relationship (business, family, romantic, friend, etc.)?*
b. *Tell me what you did say and how you said it (location, timing, mode of communication, etc.).*
c. *Tell me what happened and how it felt to do this.*
d. *How did you manage to tell them how you felt? Was it scary?*

3. Stories of Restoration

What others told you: *Tell me about a time that someone told YOU something that REALLY made a positive difference to you. What was one of the most wonderful/meaningful/significant compliments (or positive/loving criticism/suggestion) you ever received? (When I think back, the number of those is very limited, but they really made an impact on me . . . even after many years!)*

a. *Who was it that gave you the compliment (coach, boss, family member, teacher, friend, etc.)?*
b. *What were the circumstances of the time you were told (when, where, how old were you, in person or not)?*
c. *What did they say?*
d. *Why did it matter?*

What you told others: *Tell me about a time that someone told you that YOU told them something that REALLY made a positive difference to them.*

a. *Who was it that told you about what you said?*
b. *What difference did it make in their life?*
c. *Do you even recall the time/place or saying it?*

I include this here because I suggest this as an exercise that YOU can do for yourself and/or those around you. As you will see, nothing provides clarity to an individual like being asked important questions and spending the time to really think about them.

Likewise, nothing bonds a team better than a group activity that generates truth and trust, the foundations of all great relationships. And, just as I did in the first page of this book with the story about my dad, *you* need to go first and need to be completely honest, transparent, and vulnerable. Try it! You will be surprised at what you learn from yourself, your loved ones, your business team, your church group, your friends, or any group seeking to build stronger relationships.

And because of this request, I received a veritable treasure trove of heartfelt responses. I have purposely left them mostly in their original format. I have removed many names and places because the situation is what is important, not the actual participants. These amazing and varied stories from real life perfectly illustrate the three main types of communications detailed above. For purposes of simplicity, we will label them as follows:

- **Stories of Regret**: A meaningful relationship where the writer wished they had done or said more.
- **Stories of Redemption**: A meaningful relationship where the write *did* say or do what they wanted to say or do.
- **Stories of Restoration**:
  - **What others told you** that materially and forever changed your life. Some were positive words, and others were challenging words, but all helped restore the writer's own confidence and mold their self-image.
  - **What you said to others** (knowingly or unknowingly) that were heard by them in a way that meant a great deal to them.

We will take a look at each one and see what steps they took or did not take from the advice in Chapters 1–5. From this, we can reflect on what influenced the outcome and what we can learn from it.

◆

Stories of Regret

Our personal health-care is similar in many ways to the care of our important relationships. All too often, we get concerned about our health *only* when something goes wrong or it is too late. Likewise, we look back on relationships and wonder if we did all we could and said all we should have to keep them healthy and alive.

Unfortunately, sometimes that retrospective rumination comes too late for multiple reasons. These reasons include procrastination, fear, uncertainty of what to say, etc. However, just like proactively taking care of our health, we *can* proactively take care of our relationships. And just like our health, if we discover things early enough and act on them, we can help cure them and nurse them back to a healthy state.

Below are several stories about wonderful relationships spoken of with fond memories. However, what these all have in common is a form of regret and a realization that it is too late to do anything about it — or is it?

Me and Grandma

I grew up about one thousand miles from my mom's family in Tucson, and while we rarely got to see her, I thought my maternal grandmother pretty much walked on water. On the rare occasions when she came to visit us or we got to visit her and my grandpa in Tucson, suddenly the house would be alive with different smells of her cooking beans and frying tortillas and making empanadas for us, and she would play card games with us and patiently teach us a few words of Spanish.

She had walked herself across the border from Mexico one day in the 1950s after growing up a destitute, illegitimate daughter of a woman who may have never married and certainly had several kids with different men. My grandma then married an alcoholic and spent her life with him raising seven kids. She had a hard life. She didn't complain, though, and she worked like nobody I have ever seen. She was beautiful when she was young, maybe four foot ten, and a ready laugher.

She worked in a department store in Tucson, and she sent us savings bonds for our birthdays. She mostly dressed simply. She was very fair skinned and kept out of the sun, and she was relentlessly clean all the time.

One day, we were riding around in her car in Tucson and she was listening to some indecipherable mariachi music in Spanish, and I didn't know a word of Spanish. I'm silent, the speakers of my grandpa's trophy Grand Marquis squawking away, and she's quiet. And then she just starts translating the songs into English, and suddenly I realized she had this whole wealth of knowledge I would never touch because of growing up "white" in Kansas City.

She came to my graduation at Yale and seemed a bit intimidated but also every bit herself. She toddled around with her little umbrella in the rain and shine and saw what was there. She met my girlfriend, now wife, when our families went out to dinner at a restaurant that stuck out a bit over the Atlantic Ocean. We brought my friend Maggie, who was estranged from her parents and who had become part of our family over the past four years.

I hope my grandma felt some satisfaction, like she was able to get to where she wanted to be when she left her shack in Mexico and started walking that one day. As I raise my own family in one of the richest counties in the USA (and thus, the world), own a business, am a college *graduate, and speak the language here with no accent . . . I have so many things that were not within her reach. **I wished I had told her "See what you did?" I didn't have the words at the time.***

*About a year later, I cried the hardest I have ever cried when she died unexpectedly from a stroke. I wasn't sad for her suffering, as there was very little, if any, and I wasn't angry that God had taken her. **I was mostly just sorry for myself that I couldn't see her anymore.** And, I still feel that way. I'm proud to be the grandson of this amazing woman—who is still my grandma—and I love her.*

This story is the reflection of a young man who lost a grandmother who was both the courageous matriarch of his family and someone he loved and respected. Could you sense the pride he feels for her achievements? His only regret is that he wished he had found the words to say "Well done, Grandma" while she was still alive.

He sees it as "not having the words," but I believe he may also have been at a loss for the time, the place, and the way to say what he wanted to say. While the pain of her absence is certainly very real, it is important for us to find a way to say what we want to say before the opportunity has passed.

My Forty-Year Best Friend

He was my best friend, my teammate, and my best man. He died of cancer two years ago. I wish I would have said "I love you, and my life was better all the forty years we knew each other." He and I were a team in college and after.

I really think we both knew how much we meant to each other. *His widow told me months later that when he wasn't feeling well and finally went to the hospital to get the*

> *horrible news—stage-four pancreatic cancer—the first person he called was me. I was at the hospital in fifteen minutes. I went to one of his many chemo treatments.*
>
> *We both knew what was coming, and it gave us time to look back, laugh, and really understand what an amazing time we had. We still say it today in my circle of college friends: "We did not get cheated in the fun department at college." I think that's why our friendships are so strong and have lasted forty years. We've all lived in other cities, but when we meet up, it's like we were never separated.*

This short story reflects the many emotions that enter our life during the illness and passing of someone who really meant something to us. Note the conflict between wishing I had said more but articulating in detail all that actually *was* said and done.

It is my guess that after thinking about all that he *did* say and do, the writer felt more at peace at the end of the story than he did at the beginning. Have you ever felt that way?

My Trainer

I had a personal trainer I met through a mutual contact. He was a former marine, and began a fitness business a few years after he left the service. At the time, I was looking for an "upgrade" for my work-outs and thought he would fit the bill.

We began a nearly two-year fitness relationship whereby we would discuss anything and everything. Our friendship grew, and I had an opportunity to help his son get accepted in a trade school he was eager to attend. This guy was extremely knowledgeable about life experiences, world events, and basic human connectivity.

He was invaluable in helping me navigate various work decisions and acting as a sounding board when important decisions were lurking. I had a period of about three months whereby I had to travel, so my work-out regimen was nonexistent during the time. Although I had told him I would be unable to come to our training sessions during this time, I learned, upon my arrival back, that I had missed an opportunity.

After returning, I called him up and said I was back and ready to begin our work-outs. He said, unfortunately, he had booked up his schedule and he didn't have any open spots. He said if things opened up, he would let me know.

*I realized, then and there, that **I had blown many opportunities to express my sincere appreciation for his wisdom and friendship and the bond we had developed.** I had no excuse other than the well-worn "I am busy and just didn't think about it." **I learned that we are never "too busy" to show our appreciation—in words and deeds—to those that make an impact on us.** If someone is adding value to your life, you cannot tell them enough how important they are to you. Otherwise, the relationship may be short lived, and it was for me in this case.*

This story is a bit more frustrating. It describes a lost relationship followed by the guilt of never having said that there *was* a relationship beyond that of client/trainer and that it meant a lot to the writer. The trainer was a person that the writer clearly respected, and was an authority on not only health, but also a great confidante about life.

His regret comes from that fact that the barriers to saying what he should were the classic societal and personal hang-ups of "it isn't a priority." As said before, it never is until it's gone, and then it seems too late. But is it?

It is interesting for me to note in this case that even today, it is not too late for the writer to correct this situation. While he might not be able to "get back on the schedule," that isn't really the issue; what he wanted to tell the trainer about the impact on his life is the issue. He really has not "blown the opportunity," and maybe *you* haven't either, even as you reflect on the relationships that ended in in a way you regret.

Never Assume

*After recently experiencing the heartbreak and tragedy at the end of a long marriage, this topic is certainly close to home for me. There are many layers of complexity that led to the dissolution. However, **one of the things my ex-wife repeatedly said to me was "You never valued me." My response at the time was "No, I have always valued you,"** and this is indeed true. But at this point, that isn't particularly credible to her. A life lesson to me coming out of this is to **be more communicative and demonstrative in future relationships.***

Here, the writer is clearly going through a difficult self-examination time following the break-up of a long marriage. As stated here, it seems that the most significant pain came from the fact that the **Fundamental Questions** of "How are WE doing, and what's that mean for me?" were never adequately answered. Also, it provides us an opportunity to reflect upon the impact of "what is left unsaid" on the relationship. As stated before, sometimes it is what we *never* speak that has the greatest impact.

Regrets to the End
When I Lost My Parents

Did I say "I love you" enough? Did I do as much as I could to make Mom's not-so-easy life (a widow at forty-two) the best I could? Since I was single, I had more to give her than my married siblings. Did I give her enough?

Mom died alone over a holiday weekend, and though all of us checked in almost daily, it was two p.m. before we realized something was amiss. So many rough patches sixteen years later. I tried to be the one who could give her nice clothes, vacations, and dinners to nice places. But in the end, I think Mom was too tired and stressed to carry on.

Dad was an amazing father who died when I was eighteen. There was a cancer diagnosis a month into my freshman year at college. We all tried to hold it together. Mom knew the prognosis was dire, but kept it from us for as long as she could. The first-semester grades came in the mail the night Dad was dying. I wanted to call him and let him know, but it was too late. He passed by the time I made it to his bedside.

We knew of his devout faith and generosity, but we had no idea of the magnitude of both. Over five hundred friends, neighbors, and family members attended his funeral. Families my siblings and I did not even know shared so much about him.

We learned from a family of the Christmas they had no money for gifts—Dad bought them presents. We heard about the time the school needed a new PA system—soon the nuns had it. We heard of the school-lunch programs Dad took care of. A humble man whose actions spoke louder than words.

*My regrets: **Two amazing people I still miss, wish I could take care of, but pray to constantly for their guidance, and to say "I love you."***

It goes without saying that so many of the stories submitted related to the loss of parents. This universal event seems to evoke almost equal amounts of regret and redemption. This story is a perfect example.

The writer extols the virtues of both of her parents. It seems that there was no slight, no unfulfilled relationship. In fact, to the contrary. It reads like a wonderful, caring, and devoted daughter enjoying a life with her loving parents.

I believe in this case, the regret is really a wish. It is the wish that her mom and dad knew of her love and respect . . . that they knew of the pride she felt about the nature of their hearts, their souls, and their unselfish actions. I do not know, but I imagine in each of her prayers, this is the wish she sends to help her attempt to find peace in this challenging world.

Lost Friends

In college I lived with friends my last two years that were like family. We really cared for each other and looked out for each other. I started going "astray" and doing things I shouldn't have done, and they called me into accountability because they loved me. I didn't receive their words well, and denied their truths to me and ended up walking away from the friendships.

I wished I had been wise enough to listen to their words of love and concern, and receive them, and change. *It would have saved a lot of hurt and pain for myself that year and moving forward.*

I didn't listen to them or receive their words due to my own stupidity and pride. I didn't come close to receiving them at all at the time . . . but now wish a million times over I had — to preserve some very lovely friendships then and now.

This writer is a classic example of someone who did not put much value in the words given to her when she was young. This was probably because even though these friends were viewed with love and respect, their authority was questioned. We all remember being young and not only thinking of ourselves as the smartest person in the room, but also felt no one else "got it" . . . so we ignored them.

With the distance of time and maturity, the regret of a lost opportunity creeps in. But, again, as you read the last line, it seems to me that perhaps it is not too late. We feel that the opportunity is lost, and the chance is past, but is that really true?

When My Best Friend Moved . . .

She was my best friend from childhood. We were inseparable from three years old through high school. Then, her family moved. I'll never forget the pit in my gut while I watched their station wagon drive to the end of the court and turn right. She came back to visit a few times. We had a few phone calls and letters. But, it was in a time that we were both just going into high school, and we tried to keep in touch but grew apart and lost contact.

My regret is that I wish we were still in each other's lives. I think of her often and fondly. She made me a better human by her continued, steady, and trusted influence in the early and formative years of my life. I wish I'd kept calling and writing and trying. I wish we both had. I love her, and the best memories of my childhood were because of her.

For years I thought of calling her. But so much time had passed; I was afraid of rejection. Then, I was cleaning out my mother's house and came across photos of the two of us together the last sleepover we had before she and her family moved to New York. I missed her so desperately, and realized how very deeply she impacted who I'd become as a person. She was motivated, smart, funny, and made me a better human by her influence. I decided to look her up on social media, expecting to find family photos and posts about food and dogs. Instead, I found her blog—her blog that was written by her and chronicled her battle against cancer.

I will never forget that moment, not as long as I live. I reached out to find her and tell her that I loved and missed her and was hoping to reconnect. That I'd never had a friend in my life who was as special or as deep of an influence as she was.

I was a year and a half too late. She had died of stage-four breast cancer before I could tell her. I sent the photos to her sister and mother on Facebook, along with my condolences. We are still in touch. But, I miss my friend. I missed telling her, and now I never could.

As young girls we had decided that we were going to be novelists. Her father was an editor for Avon books and was editor for Watership Down, the author Fern Michaels, and many others. We had an "in." So, we both wrote silly fan fiction based on Battlestar Galactica and Star Wars.

Ultimately, she became the writer. Her writing changed lives. It changed mine. I poured through her blog for two days. Sobbed my way through it, really. She told me her story there. She taught me again not to take for granted the sun on your face on a cloudless day; to drive with the windows open and feel the wind in my hair. She made me smile.

She told me on other days how very lonely she was because cancer had an unexpected responsibility: to make everyone around her feel better about the expiration date on her life. Post after post, she told me of her courage and struggle and joy and fear, right there on the page in her own words. But she would never hear mine. She would never hear that I was sorry. That I loved her. That I missed her.

> *. . . Or that she had managed to continue to make me a better human by telling her story. It inspired me to say what needs saying when it needs saying. She taught me that in life and beyond life, kindness and truth and beauty are the things, in the end, that truly matter.*

We've all had the experience of saying goodbye to a childhood friend when their family (or ours) moves away. It seemed like the end of the world. How could this happen? Why can't we all stay together? Painful childhood memories that are accompanied by firm and resolute promises to "write each other every day," "stay in touch," and "always be friends," all meant to be true, but promises that are very difficult to keep literally.

This story is about one of those wonderful relationships, the years together, the move, the loss of contact, and the random act that made her decide to reach out after all these years. What happened next is the best testimony of why we all need to pause once in a while and take inventory of our relationships. Have we told those we care for how much they mean to us? It's painful when we don't.

Grandpa

My grandpa passed away somewhat suddenly back in 2004. He was a bit older, but was still very active. Late in life he was an avid tennis player, frequent golfer, and a late-life runner. In the winters when he could not run or bike outside, he would run five miles a day by running circles in the basement of his duplex. He was an engineer at Bendix. While I'm not sure what his title was, I always looked up to him and called him a rocket scientist. My grandpa was also a huge sports fanatic and worked in different coaching roles for forty-plus years.

I remember him so fondly, and I think I got a lot of who I am from him. *My desire for competition, love of sports, my straight and direct approach, my willingness to help others, my passion to work hard every day, even if nobody really sees it, my love of tinkering on electronics, my disgust with paying others to do something around the house that I could do myself, etc., etc.*

He was always there for me and, like most kids, I took it for granted. **I assumed he would always be there** *to play golf with me, to teach me how to solve my algebra equations, to help me work on my pitching, to go to the movies with, to teach me how to perfect my ping-pong swing, to help me raise my kids, etc., etc.*

Maybe I'm overthinking it, or more likely, it's just bringing up a lot of great old memories of my time with him. **It breaks my heart to think that I never stopped to tell him how much I love him, how much I appreciate the time we spent together, and how I have modeled my life after him.** *It seemed insignificant at the time. I mean, he knew, right? Maybe, but not stopping and telling him hurts. I don't know if verbalizing it to him would have changed our relationship, but it certainly would've helped me feel better now that he's gone. I'm sure* **there are times when telling someone you love them is for the receiver, but with his passing I realized it can also be just as important for the person talking.**

Thank you for the questions and for helping remind me to pause and remember my grandpa.

This is the poignant story of a man who lost his grandpa thirteen years ago and the sting of regret is still there. I believe this story brings up three significant lessons for us:

1. This man was someone who was loved and respected and an authority. He certainly qualified as a person who truly means something to us.

2. It seems the more we rely on and revere someone, for some reason, we add more immortality to that relationship. How could it ever end? Especially when we are young, we don't see either departure or death as a possibility. Therefore, why say it now?

3. But, it is in his next-to-last paragraph that he really teaches us a lesson. We do not need to tell others how we feel *only* for them. Indeed, especially for stories like this, we tell them for *us*, because we are the ones who will mourn the loss.

The Story of Kevin and Mike

Kevin and Mike were more like brothers than friends. Confidantes, co-conspirators, family. The stability that kept me fairly sheltered from the angsty, emotional turbulence of high school.

I texted Mike the other day "IS IT THE SHOES????", as although we live in different cities, our banal sense of humor carries on like no time has passed.

I last spoke with Kevin in 2008.

From freshman through junior year of high school, we spent almost every waking hour together, serving as the backbones of one another's lives. Kevin and I actually attended the same school and were part of the same youth group. We played the same sports, liked the same music, lived the same lifestyle. God, I loved that fucking guy!

Sometime around senior year of high school, Kevin gradually started drifting away. There is no watershed moment or catastrophic event that defines the end, rather a gradual and imperceptible erosion of the bonds that linked us.

We had assumed he had just gotten lazy, didn't like to party anymore . . . Who knows? Things were still great when we were around one another; it just wasn't as often as it used to be. I figured everything was fine.

Morgan Freeman narration Everything was not fine.

College brought about almost complete radio silence. I again didn't notice, as I lose touch with a lot of people when we are in different cities, and I was wrapped up in my own new life.

Fast forward to 2008. Kevin had moved to Canada in 2005, and I hadn't spoken with him since. None of us had any idea what fully transpired, and mostly thought it was his doing. As much as it sucked, our emotional IQ and empathy was just a shade above nonexistent at that point, and we mostly shrugged it off. I got a call from a mutual friend in 2008 that Kevin was in town and would go out to lunch with the three of us.

I can't say that my reaction was mature at that point, or that I was as fazed as I am now, looking back. Kevin revealed that he had felt replaced by another guy we became friends with. That he felt there was no room in our lives for him anymore. My response to such a depressing revelation was layered with defensive posturing and accusations. Perfect. **At the time, I needed to be right,** *to prove I had nothing to do with him feeling like our blood-brotherhood had been severed.*

Ten years later, as I ponder for the first time in years what transpired, I'm moved to tears thinking of my actions. Was I at fault? Did I really "replace" him? Was he being irrationally paranoid? **The correct answer at this point is "What difference does that make?"** *I had a friend who was composed of my same spiritual DNA, and I haven't spoken with him in ten years.* **Who gives a shit why or who's at fault?**

> *Looking back, **I have no idea if I ever told the guy how much I loved him.** How he literally forged the man and father that I am today. How much I owe him and Mike for the countless days and hours they spent dealing with my often-times train-wreck bullshit and still walked by my side. I didn't need to tell him these things, though, because he already knew.*
>
> *Did he, though? Did he think we replaced him as a friend at one of life's most fragile junctures because we loved him?*

This is the only story where I have kept the names because this is a story from my son, Adam. We all loved Kevin and Mike, and it was not easy to read this story, but it is important to learn from all the situations you can, hard as they might be.

I was most moved here by his reasons for NOT saying what Kevin wanted and needed to hear. It goes back to Chapter 3, where we talked about our own fears and insecurities getting in the way of true communication. In this case, it was his need to be right that overpowered even his ability to hear what Kevin was saying. But, the true realization is the "What difference does it make?" statement he makes. While that is difficult to do in the moment, it is with reflection that we often can't even remember what the disagreement was all about. All that we do remember is the dull ache of a damaged or lost relationship.

Notice also that Adam's final reflection is wondering if he ever even told Kevin how much he meant to him. As I read this, I am beginning to observe a possibly encouraging trend to the regret stories. Maybe it is NOT too late to change the **Stories of Regret** to **Stories of Redemption.** Can you imagine how Adam would feel if he made the commitment to find and tell Kevin what Kevin needs to hear and what Adam needs to say?

My Mother

She was my rock, my world, my best friend. She dedicated and sacrificed every single moment of her life to make sure I was taken care of. She dreamt her whole life of having a daughter, and when she had one, she put every ounce of effort to ensure that I had a good life, regardless of how nonglamorous it would ever be.

She worked three jobs to provide food on the table and gas in my car. I never had nice things, but I had clothes on my back and a fun, simple life with her.

What I didn't realize is that I took advantage of her. I would make dumb teenage decisions, talk back, and do just about whatever I wanted to. Without fail, she was still always there for me.

What I know now is that woman was letting me live my life. She wanted me to experience things so that I would, at some point, realize the difference between what matters and what doesn't.

*As she got sicker and weaker, I felt this overwhelming feeling of helplessness and dependence on her presence that I for so long ignored or discounted. I started to realize that as much as I thought I would have her forever, now I wouldn't any longer. When she was taking her final breaths, I said to her, "**I love you. I will always miss x, y, z. I will be okay. You can go now.**"*

These all seem selfish now.

What I should have said to her was "Thank you." *Thank you for loving me and raising me right. Thank you for showing me what it looks like to put the people you care about first. Thank you for showing me what it means to work hard, love hard, and make a family for yourself. That you don't need a man to make you happy, only yourself. Find something that inspires you and go for it. Don't settle. Be kind. Be generous. Be humble.*

> *I wish I would have told her how impactful she was to me.* **She deserved to know how influential she was, and I just assumed she did.**
>
> *What this has taught me is to live in the moment and make a point to tell people how important they are.* **Remind the people you choose to spend your time with that they are special, appreciated, and loved.** *You never know if you won't have the chance tomorrow.*
>
> *Through my experience, I try to demonstrate loyalty to my friends and commitment to my work ethic. I truly feel that the most productive companies are a family. They communicate well, are group-oriented, and encourage feedback. You never know what is going on in someone else's life. Therefore, I make it a point to engage, ask questions to show support, and show my appreciation for their hard work.*
>
> *Treat every day and every relationship as a gift!*

This is an interesting dual-emotion story. This person obviously cherished her mother and felt some remorse for having been a typical teen. However, she seemed initially comforted by the fact that at the end, she told her mother that is was okay to let go, and that she loved her.

The interesting part is in the statement she made, "That seems selfish now." It is with maturity that we all come to realize that grieving, loss, and sadness are mostly visited on the remaining survivors. What this writer realized is another way of saying the **Platinum Rule**. In this case, she now changed her "motive" after her mom died. It went from "letting her go" to wishing she had really thanked her for all she did. This is truly saying what THEY would have you say to them.

Lessons from Stories of Regret

As I spent more time with each of these stories, all relating to regret, I noticed several themes in common:

1. In most cases, the notion of regret was amplified by the thinking and reflecting that this exercise forced them to do.
2. In most cases, there is still time to change the outcome, but in only one or two cases did the person resolve to do so or actually do so.
3. In most cases, after it is too late to change the outcome, most people seem 100 percent capable of articulating the exact message they wish they had said. I believe that still brings some peace to them, even if the message has to be delivered via thoughts and prayers versus in person.

What do these stories tell us, and what can we learn from them? I believe key takeaways are:

- Resolve to spend time reflecting on our past relationships. It seems that whatever regret came from how they ended, there is a positive value in thinking about the *entire* relationship and putting the end and the regret in context.
- If there is nothing that can be done to change the outcome, then take the time to create the words that you wish you would have said, and SAY them, if only to yourself, because remember, for many, these "words that matter" serve to salve the wound of regret of the speaker, and sometimes that's enough. While it may not help the relationship, per se, the memory of the relationship is made better by the one who remains behind.
- If there is still time to shift the dynamic of your relationship from regret to redemption, then go back to Chapters 1–5 and work out the why (motive) and then the what, where, how, when, and make amends.

I just listened to my daughter-in-law this morning say the most profound thing to my four-year-old granddaughter. It seems that my granddaughter had a spat with a young friend at preschool and had vowed never to speak with her again.

Her mom told her, "I understand just how you feel, but when I was little, my sister—your Auntie Jo—and I fought all the time. What if we had never made up? Think of all the fun times and love we would be missing, and you would never have known her or your uncle or cousins. Wouldn't that have been sad?" My granddaughter agreed that yes, that would have been sad.

If it seems so obvious to a four-year-old when told by her wise mom, it should be something that you can see and change to avoid "missing all the fun" that comes with a significant relationship.

♦

Stories of Redemption

These are the stories that we truly treasure, the ones where a potential disaster is avoided, a relationship is saved, and a life is impacted in a very positive way. While the payback exhibited in these stories is obvious and immense, the courage required to execute each one is formidable.

It is easier to *see* something than it is to *say* something. We go through life observing, feeling, and thinking about everything around us. It is those times that we act on one of those things—to say the things that need saying—that truly define us. In retrospect, these actions are labeled heroic and brave. However, in real time, they are labeled as risky and perhaps unwise.

The following stories are recalled by those who lived them, sometimes years ago, as among the most formative and life-changing events of all.

The Cool-Kids Table

I was born in Australia and moved to the US around age eight. We lived in a rough part of town until I moved to very rural town in sixth grade. I had adopted a pretty urban style of dress/speech/attitude, and didn't make very many friends at the new school. I continued to run with my friends from the city, loosely gang affiliated, and I represented that pretty strongly at school.

Predictably, this led to a bad (and not undeserved) reputation as a "thug." By the time I hit high school, my group of friends and I were stealing cars, breaking into houses, etc. virtually every weekend. Beginning of my freshman year, we burglarized a police officer's house and stole their service revolver. One of my friends brought it to school with the intention of pulling it on an older kid. This got out and the police came, arrested my friend at school, and questioned me. I ended up with some in-school suspension but that was it, aside from the furthering of my bad reputation.

My parents saw what was going on, and one thing they did in an attempt to course-correct me was to mandate that I play three sports from eighth grade on, so that I had less time to associate with hoodlums. This was fine in eighth grade and my freshman year. Despite not being previously exposed to sports, I took to them quickly.

Through freshman and sophomore years, I had literally no friends at school—complete outcast. I ate lunch by myself, got into lots of fist fights during and after school, etc. Freshman year, I got jumped in the lunchroom by a couple of seniors, nobody helped, and I ended up back in suspension for vigorously defending myself with a chair.

Sometime during my sophomore year, a guy in my grade from the football team named Mike approached me and asked if I wanted to sit with him at lunch. Mike had tons of friends, *was popular and funny, had lived in the area since birth, and was as socially connected as anyone else. He invited me to Young Life. He invited me to dinner, group movie nights, parties—everything. **He singlehandedly moved me from loner status to one of the "cool" kids** in the course of a couple of months. If not for him, I would not have met my wife. I cannot think of a bigger turning point in my life. **We are still friends to this day, but I have never thanked him for what he did.***

*So, to make a long story longer, **I am having lunch with him tomorrow.** I am going to thank him for what he did and ask him why he did it. I don't even know that he will remember it. I will let you know how that goes.*

♦

As promised, here is an update on things . . .

First, the lunch with my friend went great. We caught up a bit, and then I trapped him in my truck and told him my thoughts on his intervention in high school, and the effect it had on my life. He said that there was no reason he decided to ask me to sit with him and his friends, but that it just came to him that he should ask me.

*Later, he sent me this text: **"I just wanted to follow-up after today sunk in. Thanks a ton for taking the time to visit with me. It's indescribable to be told you made a positive impact on someone's life.** I know you can relate to being hammered by clients and staff, so today was quite a treat. Thanks again and looking forward to another lunch."*

Overall, it was a really good experience and took a lot of weight off me that I hadn't realized was there. I had been intending to talk with him about this for a long time.

This is one of the most impactful stories you will see here. It seems to have it all: the reflection of a prior life path that was changed dramatically by a single intervention; an identification of the value of that relationship decades later; the realization that you never told them; and the decision to do so. The resulting reward is obvious and should serve as a model to us all.

There is quite a lot to learn from this story. Let's look at the components. The young man who reached out to our troubled writer was certainly an authority (i.e. cool kid), but he does not meet the definition of "respect" or "authority" to the writer since he hardly knew him. But, the request to have a seat was not too much of an ask, so fortunately, the writer took a chance and it worked out.

The writer's previous failure to communicate was a function of his rebellious activities, and those all cried out for attention and the need for belonging, even to the wrong group.

But, once he knew the answers to the questions "How am I doing with you, and what does that mean for me?" from the cool kids, he could focus on a more positive direction. What he found was that initially they respected his athletic prowess, and that got him to the cool-kids table. But, it was his latent character that got him friends, a future wife, and a successful life.

Finally, unlike others we have read previously, the reflection in the exercise led him to action: not to accept regret. And the results, as you read, were surprising and powerful.

I Used My Words

I was in a romantic relationship that had its fair share of ups and downs. For some time, I only focused on the good and tried to avoid or ignore the challenging times. However, I finally found the courage to reach out for counseling and address the situation. Instead of tiptoeing around difficult issues that bothered me, **I used my words and talked to the person about what was bothering me.**

> *It was very hard to do, as I'm a people pleaser and don't want to upset the apple cart. The information was not initially received well, but later **drew us and our relationship closer.***
> *Was it scary? Of course! Very!*

This is a redemptive story of bravery and faith that led to a positive outcome. Clearly, the writer respected and loved the other party. Also, because of the depth of their relationship, there was commitment. So, this was clearly a powerful communication to be contemplated. It was loaded with all the described societal and personal fears that needed to be overcome in order to speak the words.

The writer had the correct motive, clearly wanting to do whatever was necessary to address the challenges of a relationship that mattered. Further, her "how" was to engage a counselor for advice and coaching on how to approach the situation.

When you don't know what to do, just make a decision to do something and then ask for help. As with my CEO peer groups, you are NOT the only one who has faced this, and looking for help is a strength, not a weakness.

When in Doubt, Go with Your Gut!

At an early age I was thrown into management with little or no training, but had a natural rapport with people based on a sincere interest in seeing people succeed. On my first promotion into management, I was tasked with holding a sales meeting with my team that would require me to run the meeting. Thus came my first public-speaking event, something that I feared more than some of my most dangerous life experiences. My boss and our CEO would be there for my presentation, adding to my now out-of-control anxiety.

> *How do I communicate the message of accomplishment and sincerity to a group of people while making the message individualized and sincere?*
>
> *Literally shaking in my boots, I strategized how best to reduce my angst. First, I thought sitting down while speaking to the group in a U-shaped seating arrangement would help. As I started the meeting dry-mouthed and sure this would be my end in management, I introduced myself. Then, relying on the actual experiences I had through actual one-on-one time together in the field, I stood up and behind each individual.*
>
> *Starting with the CEO, I placed my hands on their shoulders and announced to the group something positive that each individual had accomplished or contributed to our overall success. I could see and feel the happiness, appreciation, and, in some cases, the surprise that I had paid so much attention to their lives. Even though the meeting was a big success and my public-speaking fears still remain,* **I better understood sincere and meaningful content would be and is paramount in relationships on every level.**

This is a classic **Story of Redemption** and overcoming fears. I seem to remember hearing that talking in front of people is one of the top-three greatest fears of humankind! How about when it is your first management job, the CEO is in the room, AND your first time talking in front of a room? This was certainly the jackpot of anxiety and fear!

The writer showed courage and, in my opinion, was able to find that courage because he was operating with a proper motive. He really wanted to share a very special message with everyone in the room, and he was willing to be the most vulnerable and the most transparent. The results speak for themselves.

A Letter to My Scoutmaster

In 2007, I started an unfortunately short-lived attempt to thank the people that have made an impact in my life. This was a year before my oldest son entered the Boy Scouts. Boys Scouts had been a very positive and impactful part of my growing up. I hadn't talked to my scoutmaster in many years, and thoughts of him and my scout troop were coming up in my mind as my son was preparing to be a scout himself.

My aunt always has a thought-provoking Christmas card each year, and in 2006 she wrote down memories about a person important in her life. She structured the letter, titled it "Memories in Sections: Earliest, Most Fun, Most Treasured," and then closed with a thank-you. I liked the format, so I made a pledge that I would start doing one thank-you a year. I picked my scoutmaster as my first.

I wrote the attached letter and contacted him to invite him to lunch. He was surprised and agreed to meet at a local restaurant. He had aged as I had, and his health was not great. We sat down, exchanged pleasantries. He looked right at me and said, "So, why are we here?"

This wasn't exactly how I thought the meeting would start, but I said, "Sir, you made a huge impact in my life, and I wanted to thank you." He wasn't a warm and fuzzy guy, but I could tell it really surprised him. We had a great lunch and parted ways.

*It wasn't but a few months later that I received a call that he was in the hospital and wouldn't make it much longer. I headed to the hospital, and when I arrived in his room I saw he was unresponsive. **His wife came up to me, gave me a big hug, and said that my letter meant the world to him and he put it on his mantle.***

*My scoutmaster passed away that evening. I attended his funeral, and the church was packed; it was a troop reunion. **I wish he could have sat there together with us to hear*** *the stories, appreciation, and love for him and the difference he made in all our lives.* *I do know he was there in spirit and that he knew and felt everyone's heart. For some reason, we don't share our hearts enough in the moment of life with the people that matter most. If we did, it would make a huge impact.*

We all want to make a difference, and I believe it is very rare that we hear that we are or have. I still have my list of people I want to thank, and I haven't written another thank-you. I wish I could give you a reason why I haven't.

I can't wait to read your book, and just writing this experience down has empowered me to start writing thank-yous. We never know what tomorrow will bring or if we have a tomorrow. I truly want the people I love and who have impacted my life to know that I love them and appreciate their help and support.

Below is a copy of the letter that I sent to my scoutmaster:

Memories of My Scoutmaster

Earliest

I believe my earliest memory would have to be my first troop meeting some time in 1976 during Closing Circle. You always gave us something to think about, and it was a time for reflection and respect.

The troop motto, "All for One and One for All," along with the Scout Oath and Scout Law—I have never forgotten these. You always made sure it was very clear that we would live up to the troop motto and that the troop was to be run by the boys.

The blue bus, it took us everywhere: swimming at the downtown YMCA, camp-outs, everywhere we went. Sometimes we had to push it up hills, but it always made it. I seem to remember you wearing a straw, wide-brim hat that had Indian beading around it as you drove us to another adventure.

Camping

You were always there . . . camping along the Levee, hiking, or making camp at the abandoned subdivision on the bluff . . . and it goes on and on. You never told us what to do; you let us lead/follow and learn from our mistakes. I can smell the Cornish hens we cooked in pit fires and the cobblers from the Dutch ovens.

I remember a particular camporee when it rained so much that all the tents were flooded, and the busses and vehicles became stuck up to their axles. I remember again pushing the blue bus . . .

Summer Camp

One of your greatest gifts to scouts like me was sharing your love for the tribe that was a part of our summer-camp experience. I remember watching my first call night and seeing Pappy with his mask, and knowing in my heart I wanted to be in the tribe.

We always stayed at Apache right next to the pool. I remember the cases of soda we would take to camp. One of the dads was the banker, and he would sit under the dining fly and diligently run the troop bank.

I have vivid memories of the dining hall, the Point, Lone Bear, the riverfront, which became the lakefront. I remember the PA system shouting, "Attention, Camp Wigwam . . . Attention, Camp Wigwag . . ." and then "Attention, Camp Lone Star . . ." I remember the campfires and singing the camp songs: "Tell Me Why" and "America." I remember hearing taps and Kate Smith singing "God Bless America."

The memories of initiation into the tribe are even more vivid: call night, work day, being on silence, making resolutions at She-She-Be, Brave Ceremony, and the cracker barrel back at the campsite.

One of my last memories of camp, which may have been my last night at Osceola, was with my best friend. The two of us snuck out of the campsite after the adults went to sleep, and we walked to the Point. We didn't take our flashlights so we wouldn't be seen. You would have thought we would have needed a flashlight to walk all the way to the Point, but I think we could have done it with our eyes closed. We sat on the Point and talked; I'm not sure what about, but as we talked, a thunderstorm rolled in over the lake with lightning that looked like a fireworks display.

At the end of camp each year I never wanted to go home. What a gift to a young boy!

Most Fun

I believe everything was fun! Building the tower swing each year was definitely a highlight. We had loaded the swing on the water company's lowboy trailer, and my buddy and I were in the front seat of your truck following the swing. As we approached the bridge, it appeared one of the arms was going to be close to the bridge. Well, it hit the bridge! Of course we were laughing, which I believe we did a lot of. After the police discussed a few things with us and we spun the arm around, we were on the road again to the exhibition hall.

This event took place after we had stopped going to camp and we were traveling to camp for Visitor's Sunday with Roberta. You know the story. I'm not sure I have laughed that hard since.

Most Treasured

I remember seeing you taking a few naps under the dining fly at camp on a hot summer day. I remember you laughing and taking many pictures. I remember being alone, sitting by the embers of a dying fire very late at night in my long underwear feeling a true sense of peace. That moment is one of a few in my life that I believe I truly felt the presence of God. That would be my most treasured memory as a boy and now as a man.

I wanted you to know how much I appreciated all you did for me and the boys of our troop. Of all the experiences in my life, scouting and being a member of our troop with you is one that shaped my life in a profound way. I try to live up to the Resolutions of My Heart that I made long ago as a boy. I made good ones because they are not easy, but I feel blessed to have them as a guide.

Thank you for also being a guide to me, and as I raise my two young boys, I realize how important scoutmasters like you are. Thank you for the love and, of course, blood, sweat, and tears. It is said that a person is made up of all their life experiences, memories, and the people they touched. My experiences with you are very much alive in me, and I hope to pass them on to my two boys and to others younger and weaker.

Thank you for your gift!
Your Loyal Scout

There are certain grown-ups that we meet in our childhood lives that become very special as role models, teachers, coaches, and caregivers. What is so interesting is that many—actually most—of these are non-family members. In a way, they are the first adults with whom we develop a grown-up relationship.

The memories of these wonderful people are of how much they taught us, how much they listened to us, how much they respected us, and how much they took care of us. Whenever we think of these guardian angels, no matter how old we are, it brings a smile to our faces and peace to our hearts.

This writer went above and beyond when it came to redemption. He was shown a great example of how to tell someone how you feel. He decided who, when, what, and how, and made it happen. The "why" was easy for him.

His story shows us that time is of the essence, and we need to act on our better instincts sooner rather than later.

Look up to People

Meaningful communication to someone or a group starts off with one's attitude. I had an experience several years ago that gave me added insight into both my attitude and communication as perceived by those I communicated with.

While biking up a difficult hill, I developed a blood clot in my right shoulder, resulting in a four-day stay in the local hospital. I couldn't get over how nice the vast team of medical professionals at this hospital treated me. In a short time, I knew their first names and we were able to share personal stories, allowing laughs as well as good-natured ribbing of sorts. My wife could not get over the fact that so many of these people stopped in to say hi over and above their normal rounds. I took the time to learn each of their names, and it was evident we all enjoyed our time together.

After being discharged and the problem was corrected, I thought about the experience and why my emotional attachment was so strong in so short a time. I narrowed it down to life in general: **"Looking up is much better than looking down."** *I was in a bed, and my physical position while speaking with the hospital staff was horizontal, and this could be interpreted in many ways. My big take on it was, we can look down on people or* **look up** *at them, thus giving them the best possible feedback on our target points, truly understanding their humanity with love and understanding.*

The basics for effective communication are not a fad. Our attitude toward people is and always will remain the basis for building relationships via communication—those that are built not on words, but compassion. This is experienced through real action, empathy, and taking time to invest in the relationship.

People understand feelings very quickly, and they are quick to understand insincerity masked behind sophisticated verbal communication. **Reciprocity is sometimes expected,**

> *but it is the individual that can communicate without this condition that will gain the most!*

Sometimes we learn the most when we least expect it. We even redeem ourselves by communicating how much people mean to us when we don't even know it. This story is a great example of that. We learn that the humility that is part and parcel of being flat on your back and looking up facilitates the **Platinum Rule**. When we are not trying to make everyone listen to us, care about us, or make us number-one, we are truly treating them the way THEY would like to be treated.

My Time with Mom

My mom passed away just last summer. During her stay in the hospital after her second serious fall, we spent a lot of time together bedside, talking about life, family, and her favorite things—things like vacations with my family and her grandkids. So many great memories. I said, "You've been an amazing mom, caring grandmother, and wife of sixty-plus years. I'm fortunate in so many ways. I love you, and I will miss you so much."

After the decision was made to take her to hospice, where she spent eleven days, I talked to her every day. I do believe she could hear me. The Holy Spirit was present, watching over her. We relived those lunches we had together, vacations, all the games sitting in the stands watching my baseball, hoop games. All of it.

I actually felt a sense of peace when she passed away. I think we covered it all, *or as best we could. I didn't leave anything on the table. I'm the oldest of three kids; I was her number-one. It was not scary at all. Like I said, we*

> *were in the presence of the Holy Spirit. God watching over*
> *us, I think that helped me say the words.*

I found this story to be similar to many of the redemption stories. The writer is able to reflect with comfort and peace on a difficult situation. Why? Because he thought he had done his best and felt no regrets. He acted when he still had the time.

The Teenage Mom

The summer I turned sixteen years old, I became pregnant. I made the decision to place my child up for adoption. It was a very hard decision to make, but at the time it was the right decision for my unborn child. It was "back in the day" of closed adoptions, so no communication or information would ever be known or exchanged by the adoption agency between myself or with the adoptive parents. I struggled emotionally after the adoption was final. I soon realized while it was the best decision for my son, what I did not realize was the degree of difficulty it would be for me.

Shortly after my son's sixth birthday, I received a call from the social worker at the adoption agency, telling me the laws in our state had "loosened up" and, if all parties agreed, it was now possible to communicate with nonidentifying letters through the agency. I needed to write the first letter to the adoptive parents and give it to the agency. After they received it, they would then contact the adoptive parents by phone to see if they were interested in communicating.

I began the difficult task of writing the most important letter I had ever written. It had to be perfect. As I read back my letter, I began to scrutinize over every if, and, or, and but, being careful not to appear threatening in any way. I must admit, the finished product was somewhat a meatless letter. I took the letter to the agency and anxiously waited to receive a response. There was so much I wanted to know. What was his first word? When did he take his first steps? How much did they love and adore him?

After the fifth day, I became impatient and contacted the social worker. Her response was simply "Oh yes, I was going to call you. I spoke with your son's adoptive mother, and she said she didn't have time." I was devastated.

That began a very dark period of my life. I kept playing her response over and over in my head. "Didn't have time"? I could understand if she wasn't comfortable, yet I did not understand why she could not write a single letter . . . if nothing else to simply state that and to let me know how much they loved him, how much love and happiness he brought to their life . . .

I began to think horrible things. I began to wonder what I had done. What life sentence had I given to him? Could she not give me the courtesy of a letter because she was abusing him? Was it emotional, physical, sexual . . .?

My life stopped. I became depressed and withdrawn, and had no one I felt I could share these fears with. I became reclusive and found it unbearable to go out in public, and had stopped menstruating. After a couple of years, I began to hope that someday he and I would meet. There was so much I needed to tell him, and so many "I'm sorrys" I needed to say. It took a lot of time, but through the hope of one day meeting him to say what needed to be said, I began the long journey of getting my life together.

Just before his eleventh birthday, I met a social worker from a different adoption agency. After telling her my story, she contacted a social worker from the agency I had placed and made an appointment for me. It was difficult to go back. All the names and faces had changed since the last time I was there. Prior to my appointment, she had contacted my son's adoptive mother. She was actually thrilled to hear we could have contact. She said she had called the agency numerous times over the years because her son had asked so many questions. To help him, she had made a duplicate of every picture she had ever taken and put them together in a photo album. Our son made all the captions to each picture. We quickly became close friends, and at the tender age of eleven, we all met for the first time. I didn't have to tell him all of the "I'm sorrys" I thought I would have to say. He was truly loved, adored, and happy.

One day, the adoptive mom told me she had never been contacted by the agency regarding the letter I had sent, or any communication. She would have wanted that for sure.

*Shortly after we met, I decided that what had happened to me should not happen to any birth mother. I sought out the social worker who had contacted me and made an appointment to see her. She no longer worked in the adoption field, which I was glad to hear. When I arrived for our appointment, I told her who I was, and she appeared to vaguely remember me. **I was given the opportunity to tell her the profound impact her actions had on my life, the importance to make her aware so that no one else would have to experience what I had.** I don't remember what her response was; I wasn't looking for an apology, I just needed her to know. **I felt it was important to stand up for myself, my son, my son's mom, and other birth moms.***

The decision to give up your baby for adoption is no doubt an extremely difficult one to make—even more so when you are a single mom who is still in her teens. This courageous mom made that decision thinking only of her child's future and giving him the chance to be happy. A few years later when circumstances created an opportunity to learn more about her son, she tried to reach out. After being seemingly rejected by the adoptive mom, she went into a tailspin that lasted some time.

However, what makes this a **Story of Redemption** is that she tried again, and it worked. There was and continues to be a healthy and friendly relationship among the son, the adoptive mother, and the writer. But, that was not the complete peace that she sought.

She decided she needed to tell the social worker who created the negative situation how her words had affected her those many years ago. Therefore, she needed to be found. She was not out for vengeance, but in the hope that her conversation would make it a lesson to not do this again. I imagine it made an equally lifelong impact on the social worker who made the error. Again, it is not about blame; it is about seeking to help others (the social worker) know what she had done and hope that others (birth moms) never had to experience the pain she experienced.

The Fortune Cookie

A fortune cookie was presented to me by an employee on her last day working for our company. The fortune inside read, "All your hard work will soon pay off." It was a powerful moment for me and one that was badly needed at the time. To this day, that fortune still appears taped inside my planner. I don't reference it often, but I know it's there.

The employee and I were on good terms and had a friendly, mostly professional relationship. We knew each other's families, but nothing in this relationship was beyond what I would enjoy with another employee. The message itself wasn't extraordinary. The timing of the message was profound.

For some months we had experienced turmoil among a few members of our staff. **One employee in particular was the catalyst for much of this turmoil.** *But, rather than* *identifying the real problem in our organization and taking action, I nibbled around the edges.*

Some might say I was passive-aggressive in my handling of the situation. Rather than addressing the disgruntled employee, I allowed the situation to fester. I found excuses for her behavior and enabled her to negatively influence others. When employees tried to share their concerns with me in subtle ways, I discounted them or looked the other way. It wasn't that I didn't care; I simply hadn't yet realized the importance of leading with intention.

The departing employee was not the sort to talk about peers or to cause trouble. She too was good at ignoring issues and creating harmony where harmony wasn't warranted. **She was an excellent employee, a keeper, the right person on the bus.** *But it wasn't her job to fix a hostile working environment; it was mine.*

During a casual conversation **as we approached her last day of work, she felt comfortable enough to tell me what she really thought about the office's culture at the time.** *She loved everything about our mission, her work, and the way I managed the business. She enjoyed coming to work (on most days), except those days that others were allowed to dictate the tone in the office. It was during this meeting that she told me these were the only times she was disappointed in me.*

She could tell I was weakened by the conversation. I realized immediately that by focusing on the one negative individual, I took away from those who deserved my attention. On her last day of work, I was given the fortune cookie with no parting words. None were needed.

Changing my behavior was not as easy as simply rereading my fortune cookie. It has taken years of reminding myself that those who work the hardest and make the greatest commitment deserve my energy and attention. Conversely, I no longer ignore anyone who is discontent.

In recent years, my resolve was tested. One very negative individual was disappointed she was passed over for a promotion. Her negativity began to become evident to the staff. Knowing that she was not qualified for the promotion, nor would she likely ever advance, I made the decision to confront the situation.

A very direct Friday-afternoon discussion became a Monday-morning resignation. Although it was never said to the rest of the staff, it was understood that the resignation was welcome, if not encouraged. To my delight, the rest of the staff rebounded within days as if they had a new spring in their step.

Never again will I defer a difficult decision when it comes to managing for the greater good of my employees. **Rather than worrying about one person, I worry about the other fifteen who love their work and the culture we've created.**

This is a classic workplace situation of "I really meant to tell you . . ." In this case, an excellent employee found the strength to tell the truth to her boss, the writer. She made the decision to leave the company, which saddened the boss, but did so in a brave and powerful way. Knowing that she was respected and an authority, she gave a gift of wisdom and insight to her friend and boss.

While it was too late to save their work relationship, it became a **Story of Redemption** and a powerful lesson learned.

The Three Amigos' Reunion

During college I had struggled to make friends. Because of this, my grades were poor. I had lost my scholarship, and I was heading down a slippery slope. In one of my measurements labs in the first semester of my junior year, we needed to team up in teams of three for lab partners. I did not know anyone in the class and was kind of looking around for someone to team up with when these two guys asked me to join them.

It turns out this was the beginning of a lifelong friendship. The two gentlemen were Gary and Don. All three of us came from very meager upbringings. Gary's mom has MS and his father was a barber. Don never knew his father and his mother struggled to support the family. My parents had filed bankruptcy the first semester of my freshman year. So, we instantly had a bond and became fast friends.

Through the next two years we helped each other not only get through our studies in mechanical engineering, but to get through life by supporting one another both emotionally and financially. All three of us made the dean's honor roll our remaining semesters at college.

Following graduation, each of us went our separate ways and began our adult life. Don moved to Houston and became a very successful engineer for a major oil company. He soon got married, and eventually had three wonderful children. Gary and I both worked for Oklahoma Gas and Electric directly out of school. I met my wife and eventually moved to Kansas City, and have been able to start, build, and recently sell a successful company. Gary married and lives in the OKC area and is now a director for Oklahoma Gas and Electric.

Prior to us all going our separate ways, we had always told each other that if there ever was a time in our life that we were in a dire situation and needed help, we could call one another and simply say, "I need your help. Get here," and there would be no questions asked. We would drop what we were doing and go. This is a rare bond among men.

Over the past twenty-eight years since graduating college, we have seen each other every other year or so and talked three to four times a year. We all went to Las Vegas in 2014 to celebrate the twenty-fifth anniversary of our graduation. On August 22 of this year, I turned fifty. Rather than an elaborate celebration, I wanted Gary and Don to come to my lake house to spend a weekend with me, as they had never been there, and I thought it would be a meaningful way to celebrate my birthday.

Don had recently divorced, but was still madly in love with his wife and extremely passionate for his grown children. You could tell he was hurting emotionally. We discussed so many details of our life, and it was as if we had never left college. **I was able to tell both of them one evening by a campfire that it was because they asked me to be their lab partner in our measurements lab thirty years ago that I have had the success that I have had in my professional and personal lives.** *I truly believe that without their friendship, my life would have turned out dramatically different.*

Before they left, we recreated a picture on my back deck that we had taken twenty-eight years earlier while in Padre Island on spring break. Ten days after this picture was taken, Don passed away of a massive heart attack alone in his apartment in Katy, Texas. I am so very grateful and thankful that I was able to tell him of the impact a simple, somewhat-random act had on my life, and how much I cared for him. God works in mysterious ways.

This story from a dear friend of mine is one of the more emotional entries received. There is no better example of being in just the right place at just the right time and saying just the right thing.

Not only did the writer discuss his past with such love and appreciation, but he also felt empathy for the challenges of one of the friends in the present. While there was not a happy ending, there must have been a sense of appreciation and grace to have been given the chance to "say my peace" while there was still time.

The One-on-One, Unexpected Thank-You

We were in Nashville for our quarterly company executive meeting three years ago, and we were taking a limo to on offsite event. I got to sit next to one of our youngest executives, and we were talking. I told him how much we liked having him at our company and how much he meant to the team. He does a fantastic job with everything he touches, and I wanted him to know that. He lit up, and said thanks and said how much he loves working at our company. He said that he loves waking up every morning and going to work. **He really appreciated hearing that,** *and made it sound like he did not get that much feedback from people. This made me realize that we need to do more praising of people just because we feel they deserve it.*

That was a learning moment for me to make sure that we are not just talking about people when they are winning awards or public recognition, but that it means more to let people know in private. Yes, **public recognition is good and makes people feel good, but I think heartfelt talks go much further.** *I am not somebody that really praises people as much as I should. At that moment with my young friend, I think it made us closer and allowed us to be more direct with each other for both good and bad things.*

We think our words don't really matter. We think that our thanks might not come across so well. We think that a thank-you is a thank-you, and all are the same. But, none of that is true.

As I stated in Chapter 1, words do matter. It matters who they come from. It matters what they actually say. It matters when and how they are spoken. Words DO matter!

This story is a perfect example of how ordinary words become extraordinary in the hearts and minds of the receiver. Again, the giver of the compliment is the receiver of the life lesson and the redemption.

Truth or Compassion: It's What Makes Us Human (and Humane!)

Some years ago, when I was regularly visiting my dad in nursing care, I had the unpleasant task of telling him his sister had passed away. When I told him the news, his face and entire demeanor exhibited the expected evidences of grief. While he had not seen his sister in some time, she was the only other remaining family member of his generation. The realization that he was the last took its toll.

My visits at that time were about once a week, and as one might suspect, the conversations were always very similar to the prior visit. After several weeks, he asked me how his sister was doing. I reminded him that I had relayed the news of her passing several weeks ago. The effect on him was identical to the first time he heard the news. I am embarrassed to admit this series of events repeated themselves at least two more times as the weeks went by. Each time, I told him the truth, and that initial grief was experienced all over again. My dad did not have dementia, so he always knew what I was saying and who I was talking about. But, he did have short-term memory issues.

Finally, the next time he asked me how his sister was, I told him she was doing fine. A peaceful look came over his face and he said, "I am so glad to hear that she is doing well."

My initial insistence on telling him the hard truth seemed to me to be the right thing to do. *How could I lie to my father? But I look back often to the "true statement" I made to my dad about his sister and realize that one attempt* *at the truth was okay. But, I needed to speak to my dad in the context of his current capabilities and situation.*

Seeing the peace in his face made me realize that words of compassion have an impact that cannot be measured. *The things we say are what make us human. We must use them in a humane way.*

Like so many of the wonderful stories submitted, this one carries its own unique message of redemption. In it, a man brings bad news to his ailing father and watches in sadness as he takes it badly. As if that is not bad enough, because of old age and memory issues, this scenario repeats itself over and over again, each time causing renewed grief and sadness to both of them. Where will it end?

When I read the decision that the son made, I couldn't help but recall the famous Jack Nicholson line in the movie *A Few Good Men* when he answered a difficult question, saying, "You can't handle the truth!"

Sometimes we have to make the difficult decision, as a human with feelings, exactly what we say or don't say to those with whom we are in a relationship. Sometimes, compassion wins over truth. The line is never clearly black and white, but as he says, the ability to know the difference is "what makes us human."

My Best Boss

A friend and former boss and I reconnected via phone, and I just told her that she was one of the best, most empowering bosses I'd ever had, and people I'd ever known, but she was also a cherished friend. That I'd learned how to be "a creative" under her wing, and nothing in my life had created the same level of sea change she had when she told me she believed in me. That she'd given me wings.

And I wasn't the only one who thought so. It had been the feeling of our whole team (all of whom I am still in touch with and had conversed with on the subject at least one time or another). We never knew how good we had it until we didn't have it with her anymore.

She was shocked, and thanked me profusely. She then proceeded to reciprocate by telling me how I'd influenced her life. We reconnected and are still in touch. It felt uplifting. It still is.

It takes courage to speak your truth into other people's lives. *Every single time I've done it, it has taken courage.* **Some people are uncomfortable expressing emotions or accepting kind words and will reject the sentiment, which feels at the time like a rejection of you.** *But, I ask you to soldier on despite the discomfort, because I believe the world is made better when people know they've made a difference.*

You never know if the truth you speak to someone of the beautiful impact they've made in **your** *life are exactly the words they need to hear at that time to get them through a rough patch or to create that "sea change" in the shifting tide of their own life. Kindness and a generosity of spirit along with the willingness to share both openly and honestly is what makes us feel closer and more connected to each other.*

It's a unique form of energy that has real power to change lives.

We all remember our best boss. But how many of us have ever told them? Can you imagine what it feels like for someone to say that you were their best boss? This seems a great example of why it is crazy to think that there is a risk associated with this. What could possibly be the risk, especially for a former boss?

Yet, even though that boss, or that person, obviously told us how much we meant to them and how gifted we were, we somehow still failed to bring ourselves to tell them in the moment.

This writer found the courage, had the resolve, and made the call. I think you might agree that it was worth the risk.

Scared Safe

She was a friend, but that's a stretch. Actually, she was the damn scariest, meanest high school classmate AND college roommate EVER!

One day on a flood-engorged river in Missouri during freshman spring break, she and her partner's canoe had overturned. They were clinging for life to a low overhanging tree, and I was trying to figure out how to talk them out of the water and back to safety.

*All my calm, proper, and earnest suggestions weren't helping, **so I changed tactics** and screamed all the mean, ugly, hurtful words she had ever used on me. It actually felt REALLY good—empowering, actually! They both crawled out of the water, up that tree, saved themselves, and over-thanked me.*

*I spoke to them in full confidence! When I saw a **change in the expressions on their faces from fear to belief, I knew they were going to do what I said** to get them out of the situation. Scary? I did back WAY up as they got closer to dry land, but offered dry towels to wrap up in. We've been the excellent friends we needed to be ever since.*

As you can see, not all words of redemption are soft and flowery. Sometimes, they are just the right words that the receiver needs to hear—whether they want to or not. In the short story above, you likely noticed many things from our earlier chapters in a small space.

The right person, delivering the right message, using words delivered in the right way. The time, the place, the discomfort . . .

all were there. Yet, the result was successful, and the long-term result was fantastic.

But, as you can also see, no one said it's easy. It is never easy, but always worth it.

Brotherly Love

When I was nineteen, I had a falling out with my biological mother. Over the last eleven to twelve years, we have not communicated, and as a result, I also lost the chance for a relationship with my younger brother. During that time, he had to grow up without his sister.

He is now nineteen himself, and one day in July he knocked on my door out of the blue. Over the past months we have spent time together and gotten to know each other as adults. We have shared some trials and tribulations we have gone through in our time apart, and are working on beginning to grow and develop a true sibling relationship. We even joined a soccer league together. It has been very exciting to open our lives and hearts to each other.

My only regret would be not pursuing a relationship during that time myself and allowing someone to dictate that connection. Additionally, I regret not being courageous enough to stand in front of a person who hurt me so deeply and stand up for my relationship with my brother.

My redemption would be continuing to build that sibling relationship and bond with my brother, welcoming him into my life and my daughter's life, and being the sister he should have grown up with.

I have recently had the opportunity to be surrounded by some special friends and business peers that taught me to stand up for myself. Also, to stand up for what you believe in and go

> *after the things you deserve personally and professionally. I*
> *hope I can continue to trust in that and grow within.*

This is a classic **Story of Redemption** that I am happy was given to me to include in this book. Most of us have the experience of losing someone for some reason during our lives—disagreements, growing apart, physical moving, or even death. While that alone is a very sad thing, the tragedy is the "collateral loss" that often accompanies such a loss. I hear of friendships lost following a divorce because of the stress of seeing one without the other. I've heard of best buddies lost because the family physically moves away, and they can't be together anymore. But, a sibling is another story. The pull to reunite is a strong one, as you have seen here.

Thank You for Your Service

When I see a serviceperson in the airport, I try to always say, "Thanks for your service." Most say thanks and are usually shy about it. I have had several conversations with people about where they are from, where they are going, what type of work they are going to do. I am always surprised when talking to somebody that they don't get a lot of people saying thanks. It is usually that they get it all at once by one person saying it, and then everyone around says something.

This is typically a stressful time for them, as they are going off to someplace to train, being deployed, or returning home to see loved ones. I think this is one that I really do for myself, as I have never served in the military. They are the ones defending our freedom, and I have never participated in that. They are coming and going from all around the world to do something bigger as I am typically

> *flying from a customer, tradeshow, or just having fun. These men and women are going somewhere they maybe have never been to protect us. Seems like they need much more thanks.*

Here we see self-reflection again yielding life lessons that might otherwise have been missed. Here we see that by being a model for others of saying the right and true thing, the result is magnified and multiplied manifold.

The compliment is more than "thank you for your service," by itself a nice sentiment. But, to treat them as real people by asking for details and background applies the **Platinum Rule** again. They need to have their mind taken off of where and what they are headed for. They need to be reminded of why and for whom they are doing it.

Again, the writer admits that perhaps the one to gain the most from this exchange is actually him.

The Destination Is the Journey

The destination is the journey. **Life is about living in the moment,** *recognizing the gifts you have in front of you, acknowledging when you are happy, and showing gratitude and appreciation for all that are around you for making that moment possible. This is the lesson I learned as an Army Special Forces officer after a twenty-one-year military career.*

In the spring of 1998, one of my best friends in the military and I were watching a moving in Aiea, Hawaii. We both were recent graduates of the US Ranger School; we were invincible and were ready to take on the world. What remains in my mind to this day is one of the opening scenes of that movie. Soldiers were riding in a US Navy beach-landing craft. The doors opened, and bullets cut down everybody in sight while the remaining soldiers struggled to get off the boat and make their way to the beach while wading through waist-deep water, a hail of bullets, mortar fire, and explosions all around them. The movie was Saving Private Ryan. *It was D-Day, and the soldiers were conducting a forced landing on Omaha Beach. At some point my friend and I glanced at each other openmouthed, as we knew a potential reality that could exist for both of us that most in that theater would never have to contemplate.*

After that movie in 1998, I decided that when I deployed to combat, I could not expect to make it home because if I did, then I might do something to save my own life. My job as a second lieutenant in the infantry was to lead soldiers and put the mission, the organization, and the needs of my soldiers above my own, first and foremost. Life could never be about me; it had to be about them.

Now, fast forward to the fall of 2004. I am a young, newly married US Special Forces detachment commander with a four-month-old son, and my unit is deploying to Afghanistan for the first time.

When I kissed my wife and son goodbye for the last time before I boarded that bus to take us to our plane, in my mind I said goodbye, and I mean GOODBYE. I never thought I would see them again, and I know my wife thought the same. At that point in my life, that was one of the hardest things I had to do.

Over my twenty-one-year military career, we have repeated that process on numerous occasions, and it never got easier, especially with four kids who were progressively getting older. Each time, I made a point to let them know what they meant to me, and wrote a letter to them the night before every deployment reiterating what I told them in the days leading up to the deployment.

*I have lost a lot of friends throughout the years, and for one reason or another, I am still here. Throughout my military career, **there were constant deployments which***

I never knew if I would return from. Through this process, I learned to recognize when I was happy, and appreciate the moments that I never thought I would be able to experience. Moments like just being with my wife as we watch our kids interact, laugh, and play with one another. That particular thought led me to appreciate more my friends, family, and those I worked with and interacted with on a daily basis. I now believe that people should be appreciated for what they do on a routine basis, even if "it's just their job." I believe everyone has a choice on the level of effort they will give, and when someone gives 100 percent and performs at the optimum level, I appreciate it because it further enables everyone around them to do the same. Through my experience, I think it's important to recognize that.

At the most awkward times, I will stop and look at everyone and say, "I am happy. Thank you." I do this so I never forget to live in the moment and show gratitude and appreciation for all those around me who are making that moment possible. I also do this in hopes that others will learn to do the same.

I am now recently retired from the military. I have been in business with some of my best friends for three years, and continue to remain connected with my friends from the past while at the same time developing new relationships with close friends as I continue with this next stage of my life. Most importantly, I am with my family on a daily basis as we fight through this life together. I am happy and appreciate all those around me, but most of all I appreciate my wife for making this all happen.

I thought it would be interesting to follow the previous story with another point of view on military service. This is from a young man who served in the military. Not only did he serve, but was an Army Special Forces officer who found himself in harm's way time and again over many years of combat deployment. This is the story of what might be going through the minds of the military heroes we see at an airport. Their pensive expressions might reflect the types of thoughts as described above by the writer.

The lesson here is to never take anything for granted. We say it from time to time as we go about our daily lives. However, when you are in the active military, you say it in a way that demands action. He learned never to take any goodbye for granted, because he knew that any of those could certainly be the final goodbye. But even now that he is out of the active military, he has carried those valuable lessons into the civilian world. Showing our love and gratitude is not only for times of crisis, but for all times.

Thank You, Bill

This one is personal because it happened to me. The event itself and the ironic happenstance of the rapid illness and death that followed it changed me as a person forever. It also changed me as a Vistage chair in a profound and permanent way.

My avocation is being a Vistage chair, whereby I facilitate monthly meetings of sixteen to eighteen–member peer advisory boards of CEOs and business owners. We've become a tight-knit family who share the good, the bad, and all because we all have so much trust and so much in common. In the lonely world of business leadership, this is a welcome "safe place" to meet, talk, and grow.

Even though most members stay on the board for quite some time, there are inevitable departures. They can be because the company is sold, change of jobs, or just not experiencing the value. In the beginning, when I was trying to build my practice, I found these departures extremely personal and painful. I always saw their departures as mostly about me and "not being enough." People would just sort of vanish, and unless someone specifically asked, I really didn't talk about the departures.

Some time ago, something happened that, while NOT planned, changed that tradition and the culture of our groups forever. A gentleman named Bill had just sold his very successful company that he had owned for decades. Bill was special to me because he was my very first boss coming out of graduate school. On top of that, when I started my Vistage practice, he was the first one who committed to me to join the group. I will never forget how that vote of confidence propelled me to keep going in building the groups.

At Bill's final meeting, I interrupted our normal agenda and told the group that each one of you will answer the following question: "What has Bill meant to this group and to you?" Additionally, you will look at him and tell this directly to him.

There was a deafening silence in the room, and it seemed like hours until someone spoke (although it was only about a minute). As soon as the first brave soul went, it was all I could do to moderate this avalanche of words, feelings, and emotions. Tears were shed, hugs were given, and at the end, I received the greatest single gift I have ever gotten. After everyone had left, Bill walked up to me, grabbed my hand, looked me in the eye, and said, **"Jeff, that is the kindest thing that has ever been done for me, and I will treasure each and every word—and YOUR part in it—for the rest of my life.** Thank you, my friend!"

Less than eight short months later, Bill had passed away. While the pain and shock of losing such a beloved friend so quickly never ebbed, the peace that I was granted from his words to me on that day were indeed the **greatest and most timely single gift I have ever gotten.**

You can imagine that when you are in a room of eighteen impressive and successful CEOs and business owners, the decision to change the topic from business brilliance and strategy to the softer area of "feelings" is a risky one. Every time I contemplate "going there," I am filled with trepidation and consider backing out. The more nervous I am, the better it works out. I am always amazed that they follow me and that they are all in!

I always thought they listened to me because they respect me and honor my authority (mostly for my business background). But, as it turns out, they really listen to me because of my **motive**, my courage to "go there," and their trust of me. Trust, as I have said before, comes from a place of transparency and vulnerability. And it was in this realization that I decided the truth I wanted to write about in this book.

It is critical for us to really think about why we are saying what we are saying and why they are or are not listening. It is this type of deep reflection that leads to the type of life-altering realization that I made in the prior paragraph. It happened to me, and it can happen to you.

When you explain to everyone that we are now going to look in the eye of someone and tell them exactly how you feel about them, that is a game changer. As it turned out, it changed for the better. As outlined in the previous story, we all benefitted from the exchange, and it added much-needed comfort in the following months. His passing was, of course and in this case, something we never saw coming, but having the experience of speaking our truth to him beforehand would prove to be an amazing blessing.

Having the ability to move the relationship from the head to the heart is the art of true communication. Bill taught me that. Thank you, Bill.

Lessons from Stories of Redemption

These stories have several observable things in common:

1. In most, the writer finds themselves in an uncomfortable situation just prior to using their words.
2. In most, the writer, upon reflection, finds that the redemption truly helped them as much as or more than the person to whom they spoke.
3. There is a true appreciation and relief from finding the courage to speak the words.

In other words, the only difference between regret and redemption is that in redemption, we find both the courage to speak and the way to speak the words. None of the results brought failure. Of course, that is no guarantee, but the odds of success are better if you try.

A friend of mine was one of the premier investigative agents in the FBI for decades. In response to my request for stories for this book, he sent the following:

I will give you a twist on what you have asked for. During the thirty years I spent with the FBI, I eventually developed an interview technique that impacted the outcome in countless investigations. My job involved getting people to tell me what they knew. At what appeared to be the end of a witness interview, in which I was convinced the interviewee was holding back, I would make some version of the following statement:

"I want to thank you for helping out on this investigation. This is an important matter, and I know it's not an easy process. But this is your chance to do the right thing and help fix a wrong. I believe you know more than you've told me, and this is your opportunity to set the record straight. I need you to make sure you've told me everything I need to hear. It's more important than you can imagine."

Probably one out of four interviews restarted at that point that otherwise would have ended. Many of those individuals were relieved to say the things they had held back. In some cases, peoples' lives were changed as a result of what was said.

I know that's outside of the examples you ask about, but thought it may have some use.

I told him that nothing could be more relevant to this book. Wouldn't it be nice if we had a "friendly" FBI agent inside our head imploring us to do the right thing and set the record straight? In fact, we do; it's called our conscience, and usually when we give it time to reflect and to breathe, it succeeds in convincing us to do the right thing. It is saying that NOTHING costs so dearly as keeping quiet, and the batting average of success for silence is zero.

Remember, all-time hockey great Wayne Gretzky said:

"You miss 100 percent of the shots you don't take."

It seems that **Stories of Redemption** are just like the many stories of success where the outcome is determined by the attitude. Whenever a relationship is threatened or damaged, there is always a way to come back. It is never over until it is over. However, when we think about the comeback, we see the following formidable obstacles:

- It has been a long time; maybe too late to fix it.
- I don't really see it as my fault; THEY should do something.
- Why can't they see that was not what I meant?
- I don't want to lose the upper hand.
- What if it doesn't work?

Sound familiar? Again, reread Chapters 1–5 to see them all and understand what it is that makes us ask these questions. It is the ability to completely recognize and then ignore all our fears and adopt the tools that give you the courage to chart a new course, try a new way, and just go for it. It is then that we "speak our truth," because, to paraphrase one of the authors, "Who cares who was right or wrong?" Redemption of the relationship is what matters, not resolution of the facts.

As time goes on, who was right or wrong should not be the question. The only questions that should be asked are, "Do I value this relationship, and how much does it mean to me?" If the answers are yes and a lot, the rest is just courage!

◆

Stories of Restoration

So far, we've covered the first two categories, Regret and Redemption, which are expressed from the initiator's point of view in each conversation. These two categories are written from the receiver's point of view.

The following **Stories of Restoration** are some of the most relevant to me, and hopefully provide evidence for the oft-stated axiom that "words matter!" I have separated these stories into two subsections.

The first are about "what others told me," again from the point of view of the listener. These are the pearls of wisdom and/or life-changing words we received from the various influences in our lives. They are a mixture of praise and admonition, all given and received with love and respect.

The second are "what I told others," and are most intriguing. We often find ourselves giving advice, counsel, and words of wisdom, and fantasize that these erudite tidbits have made a seminal impact on the life of those fortunate enough to have heard them. However, as the stories reflect, all too often the things people remember the most and that impact them the most could come from an utterance or a modeling that we don't even remember.

What Others Told Me

This is the first of three stories where someone who was both respected and had authority said something to the writer that could be considered "tough love." However, it stuck in their memory as a valuable piece of advice that still reflected respect for the relationship.

Tough-Love Story #1

Sports has always been a big part of my life, and the competition and teamwork that goes into it is something that still gets my juices flowing to this day. That is why I love where I work, because we emulate that same environment in everything we do. So, my story comes from high school basketball and my coach.

Early in the season, I twisted my ankle and was diagnosed with a high ankle sprain and was supposed to miss most of the season. I wasn't really going to stand for that, so I rehabbed as fast as I could and got back on the floor much earlier than expected—and much earlier than I should have.

When I make my return, I have this huge brace on that has metal splints up the side, so I can barely move and turn on the left leg. My first game back was a bit of a struggle moving around, but I managed. I played limited minutes, but still tried to play like my normal self. I was our point guard, team captain, and the guy everyone looked to in order to get us fired up or calmed down, depending on the situation. I was the extension of the coach on the court. We had a great relationship. He called me in for meetings with just me and asked my opinion on things, but also expected more from me, which I loved.

I was dribbling the ball up the court in that first game back, and the guy guarding me picked my pocket at about half court really easily. I was still rusty, and it showed. He went down and shot a lay-up. My coach instantly called a time-out and started going off on me in the huddle. I think your natural reaction in that situation is that you are hoping to get some slack because you were coming back from an injury and that had never really happened to you before. The reason I chose this story is for what my coach said to me in that huddle in front of our whole team, the crowd, the other team, etc. He said, "You're the point guard. Handle the (bleeping)

> *basketball, it's your job. You're the leader of the team,*
> *do your job."*
>
> I wasn't mad at all. He was right. I expected to be held to
> that standard; I wanted it. It was my job, and I failed on that
> particular instance. **I just loved that feeling of 100 percent**
> **accountability for my team and my coach. That is what**
> **gets me going in life:** *having that responsibility for leading*
> *and helping others.*
>
> This mattered so much to me because I have carried that on
> into the business world. It's my job to lead in my current position.
> Others expect me to lead, and I love that. It's a great feeling!

In this first story, a coach confronts the writer and "tells it like it is." There must have been a great relationship there, because the writer could have taken this very badly and started being the victim. In fact, it served to compliment the writer. Being reminded of his leadership role re-engaged him and brought back that accountability for himself and for the team as its leader.

While this book is about 100 percent unconditional positivism, let's use this as an example of how broadly this definition can be expanded. However, let's also remember that the receiver will always reflect on the quality of the relationship, the motive of the speaker, the appropriateness of the statements, and the time/place of giving it.

In this circumstance, the coach got it right and the player used his correction to promote the leadership training that has brought him to amazing levels of success in his life and career since that day.

> ## *Tough-Love Story #2*
>
> I had secured my first job out of college in sales, and
> reported to my first day in a brand-new city a thousand miles

from home. My boss was a grizzly veteran of the business, having been in it for thirty years. Being new, I was going to be in training mode for two years before I was fully unleashed to the marketplace.

I was assigned a mentor by my boss who was a guy who had great success in the business. He was technically astute, customer focused, and a very good teacher of the trade. Early on, I was eager to listen, take advice, study, and generally follow him around as he showed me the ropes.

After about six months of the mentoring, I started to believe that I was ready and didn't need the constant advice, strategy talks, product and service briefings, etc. So, I began to push back, act like I knew it all, and generally carry myself as a "green" prima donna even though, looking back, I didn't have a clue what success in sales was, because I hadn't sold a thing.

I began missing training sessions with my mentor, giving excuses why I couldn't go with him that day (I wanted to make my own calls), and generally being a total non-team player. Finally, my mentor had had enough, and he went to my boss and told him so.

Upon arriving one morning into the office, I hear my boss scream out my last name and say, in no ambiguity, "Get in here!" I thought, Uh oh, I must have really screwed up. I *arrived in his large office and he said, "Sit down and shut up. I am going to tell you why I am mad at you, and you are going to listen to every word I say."*

He proceeded to dress me up and down. Told me my behavior was disrespectful, that I was likely to fail in this business because of my attitude, that my college degree was on paper, but my career was real life, etc. To this day, I have never had a person talk to me that way . . . nor at the same time have a bigger, more positive impact than almost any communication since.

After his tirade, he calmly said, "I hope I have gotten through to you, son. *You see, many men have come*

> *through those doors, and most have failed. **I do not waste my time with the ones for whom I don't see potential.** Our corporate office sends us new grads every year, and I am usually not impressed with any of them. But, you have the ability. I can see that. I see your desire for success. Your problem is, you know it. Until you learn to be humble, admit what you don't know, and be open to advice, counsel, and help, your potential will be wasted."*
>
> *He told me to always remember that while formal education has an end, life learning does not. **You must remain in student mode as you continue to achieve another rung on the success ladder.** And if you ever find yourself leading others, remember what this experience was and take it with you, so that your followers will be humble as they begin their careers.*

This is another version of a not-so-soft presentation of words, but shows another technique used by the boss that worked. In this case, the boss was most certainly in a position of authority to the young man. However, there is no evidence that their relationship was one of depth, respect, or love at the time he spoke.

What he did was very clever. He chewed out the young man and *then*, at that moment, told him why. Once he explained his motive and the reason behind what he did, the young man A.) received the criticism in a much more balanced manner, and B.) certainly respected and found affection for the touchy boss who just said he really cared.

The respected Norman Vincent Peale once said:

"The trouble with most of us is that we would rather be ruined by praise than saved by criticism."

Again, I am not arguing for the "balanced" approach. I still do not want to bring back the word "but" at the end of a compliment. However, what we are seeing in this story is something different.

A boss decided that he wanted to have a lasting and valuable relationship with the young man. However, the young man didn't know this. In fact, he probably thought the opposite and expected shallow criticism. The boss gave him the honest truth, and instead of saying "but," put it in the context of *why* he is saying this. THAT is why the young man listened and why the message still resonates after all these years.

Tough-Love Story #3

*The best thing that someone told me that I didn't know that I needed to hear was about fifteen years ago. I was twenty-eight and working for a company, and the owner at the time, Joe, was telling a story to a small group of associates and me, and I interrupted him. He firmly yet politely said, "Excuse me, I wasn't finished," and put up his hand to gesture for me to hold on. Embarrassed for being called out, I shut up and stood there. **Afterward, he explained to me why waiting your turn is important (respect for other person, practice patience), and I have never forgotten this day!***

What humiliated me for a moment has stuck with me since that day. I appreciate that he had the courage to correct me, which in the long run made me a better listener because I realized that I would have my turn to talk, but that I didn't need to interject during someone else's turn to be heard.

This third and final tough-love story is very short, but also shares a powerful message. If you care about someone, tell them how you feel directly, specifically, and immediately. Your authority, which is already established, gives you the right to do that, but your follow-up of "why" you did this gives you the respect that makes for a lasting relationship and fond memory.

I'm guessing that if asked, Joe would not even remember this moment, where the young person he spoke to would remember it for fifteen years . . . and probably forever. What we say does matter; it doesn't matter when we said it. It doesn't always matter when we want it to, and sometimes it matters a lot when we didn't want it to.

The leadership lesson is best taught in a quote from noted organizational-behavior consultant Margaret Wheatley, who said:

"Leadership is a series of behaviors rather than a role for heroes."

It doesn't happen in sound bites and headlines; it happens in the day-to-day, even minute-to-minute behavior we model.

Midlife Sunshine

A friend/mentor was encouraging me in my job/career search, and verbally talking to me about the situations that had led up to my current search for work. I was in my fifties. They helped me do an inventory of my skills/gifts, and then pointed out the positive traits I could offer many people/companies.

I had been in a negative, beaten-down situation and needed a ray of hope! *My friend/mentor gave me much more than a ray of hope; they gave me an entire sunshine!*

This was a very simple story about communication. The friend/mentor cared enough about the writer to find the courage to encourage her. I don't know how hard it was for him to recognize and act on this, but I do know that it made all the difference to the writer. Again, we don't know if the friend even recognized it as such, but the receiver certainly did.

Isn't this what it's all about? If our unscripted and unintentional moments can have this much impact, imagine if we approach our important people and important conversations with intention. This kind of impact has ripples that can spread across families, organizations, cultures, and countries!

Knowing this, why would any of us ever hesitate to express true, kind, and necessary words to those around us?

Coaches Know Best

Two of the most memorable moments in my life where someone did tell me both were with coaches. One was my soccer coach, Dale, and the other was a basketball coach, Tim. While the exact words are forgotten, both comments made me feel the same way. Each coach independently let me know that A.) they expected something from me, and B.) they knew I could deliver it.

*Both coaches may have been full of crap, but I will never forget how it made me feel and how it made me better. **Their belief in me led me to believe more in myself than I would have otherwise, and, in turn, I performed better.** It also motivated me to be a coach, but I never knew how to do it until recently I got another nudge . . .*

I was amazed at how many stories and memories touched on coaches and athletic endeavors. The coaching relationship is a unique one. There is no doubt that there is authority and commitment on the part of the coach. It is never clear to me if there is the respect/love that makes for a highly influential relationship.

I think there is certainly MORE desire of this on the player's side, as we all want to please and have a special relationship with our coach. It is likely not possible for that to be reciprocated on the coach's side for everyone. I'm sure there are exceptional examples, but it would be very challenging.

But, it does mean that words spoken by coaches in our past lives seem to carry an extra level of strength and veracity as we grow older.

Man of Few Words

My dad said something that blew me away. But first, some background. My dad was an all-American basketball-and-track guy in college. He's in the college's Athletic Hall of Fame. I idolized him, and always worked hard at my sporting crafts because of him. I wanted to be that good (although I was not even close). However, the most interesting thing is that he never pushed me to participate. He never coached me on car rides home after a game, critiqued my skills—none of it.

It was near the end of my senior year in high school. We had a good basketball season. Also, in baseball, we won the state title and I got selected to the city all-metro team in basketball. We were packing up at the gym after our last game when he came up to me, put his arm around me, and said, "I'm really proud of you." **I always wondered if he was really watching closely at the games. This was validation that he very much was.** *It was an amazing moment for me, an emotional one, too.*

Scott Eastwood had this to say about his famous actor and father, Clint Eastwood:

"My old man is a man of few words."

It appears the writer in this story would say the same thing. But, as is often the case, when it comes from someone who we admire AND who has authority over us (as this dad obviously does), it matters. Like a parched man in the desert, we seek the meaning of each and every utterance because these words are not shared as often as they could be.

It never hurts to communicate a bit more. At least until you have given the answers to our **Fundamental Questions:** "How am I doing with you, and what does that mean for me?"

Twenty-Five Years Later . . . Words Matter

One of the most significant things ever said to me—or in this case, written to me—was from my dad in his early eighties.

My dad left our family when I was in ninth grade under very difficult conditions. I was the youngest of four children. My older brother (nine years senior) and sister (seven years senior) were out of the house; my other sister (two years) and I were still at home. My mother had just survived a surgery for colon cancer that no one predicted she would. We just got her home to recover, set up a hospital bed in our living room, and my older sister sat out a semester at OSU to care for her.

My dad came home and announced that he was leaving the family for a woman he was currently having an affair with. At the time, he said that he realized he may lose his family, but that was okay with him. The other woman had already left her husband of around thirty years and moved to our town, based on the prediction my mother would not make it through her illness. This was incredibly painful from the onset and during the years to follow. However, it seemed that Dad was oblivious to the consequences of his choice.

Approximately twenty-five years later, a letter showed up with an article from the Wichita Eagle and Beacon *where a dad had told a story about taking his son back to the airport to return him to his mother at the end of his summer visit. On the way, his dad wanted to talk to his son about God, which resulted in his son making some negative comments about God. This made the dad realize that it was easier for his son to be angry at God than to be upset with his dad about his divorce and resulting broken family. The dad in the story relayed about the waning minutes he had with his son in the airport, stroking his hair before he put him on the plane. His admonition was to never visit this on your children.*

My dad's words were simple: **"I read this story today and it made me cry. I'm sorry."** *That meant more to me than anything he ever did.*

There are few more powerful connections in our lives than that of our mother or father. This story about a boy's loss of his father to a broken marriage is poignant. The tragic facts of the entire situation help to illuminate the depth of sadness (and possibly anger) this boy felt toward his father.

The courage (or at least guts) the father found in sending the story and note helped the young man in a meaningful way that still resonated with him today. We don't know if the dad ever knew it, or if he even deserves to know it, but the act of doing it was an action of courage.

The Gift of Humble Words

I think words are important. They may feel sort of elusive, kind of intangible, but words are what we use to have a conversation, craft text messages, and create something like this book you're holding. Words are what we use to start, grow, or end relationships. I think words make up some of our deepest realities. And, that may be why words stick with us.

For me, the words that have been the stickiest, the ones that have impacted my life the most, were words of humility. We think that to be impressive, to make an impact, our words should be well-crafted, novel, and powerful. But, I don't think we could ever overestimate the power of words of humility.

*Growing up, if my dad made the wrong decision or raised his voice, he would apologize to me. **Can you imagine what hearing "I'm sorry" from my dad did in my head and heart as a little girl?** I felt cared for, thought of, and considered. I may not have understood why it was so impactful back then, but now I understand that his apology was him laying down his pride to tell me how much he loved me.*

Words of humility are challenging to string together sometimes—apologies probably being the toughest of them all. But, the phrases "I'm sorry," "I don't know," and "Me too" are just a few words each, and they're oozing with humility and could become some of those forever-remembered, sticky words.

On a more positive note than the prior story, again we see that the words and teachings of a father or a mother are among the strongest. This is because they usually rank at the very top of a young child's measures of "love and respect" AND "authority and commitment." To that, I would add BELONGING. Every human being longs to be seen, understood, and to belong somewhere. This basic human need is never more important than in the nuclear family.

This writer was most impressed when this powerful voice in her life would utter words of humility. Rather than the words of a hero, her dad's were the words of a servant leader. He taught her that humility (like saying "I'm sorry") was the glue that held relationships together.

She learned that it is not important who is right, but who shows their love first. That allows the other to accept it. If both wish to be right and no one opens up with words of humility, the relationship cannot recover.

Who, Me?

About four years ago, I was approached by the editor of a magazine in my hometown that had just started a new spin-off magazine with a target audience of fifty-plus-year-olds. I was asked to write an editorial column highlighting the magazine's focus that month, i.e. fitness, elderly parents, etc.

*I had no writing experience and asked, "Why me?" She said she was a Facebook friend and **liked my sense of humor and positive slant,** and obviously I fit the demographic and was somewhat known in the community. The magazine only published for two years and I wrote twelve editorials, as it was bimonthly. Having a deadline for work expected is something I hadn't experienced in decades.*

*I had so many people comment positively on my columns, and I enjoyed writing them more than I could have imagined. **Out-of-the-box experience that came out of thin air and was out-of-this-world fun!***

When others see something in us that we might not see, it feels great! But, only if they dare to say it. And remember, it means so much more when it comes from someone that you both respect *and* who knows what they are talking about. THAT feels amazing.

However, in the above short example, I am troubled by this question. If this person had such a gift for writing, as evidenced by this stranger seeing the work on Facebook and reaching out, why hadn't anyone before? Where were the Facebook friends or her family? Had they told her how they felt, but failed to make an impact because they didn't have the authority to have that much impact on the writer? Or, had they only silently appreciated—even envied—the writer and kept their compliments to themselves? We will never know, but this story provides another admonition to be conscious of other's gifts and talents, and "When you see something, say something!" You never know.

Who hasn't heard the legend of how Harrison Ford was cast in his career-making role of Han Solo of *Star Wars*? At the time, he was doing carpentry work, but apparently good fortune and producer George Lucas's good eye produced a different outcome.

You never know when your dream will present itself to you. You only have to know a great opportunity when you see it!

Uncle's Gift

I grew up in a middle-class neighborhood in Chicago. I came from a family of six kids with doting parents who did an amazing job at managing the household while at the same time raising us to become good and decent people. And if it takes a village, then our local church and school were also strong influences in shaping our young lives. By all accounts, we kids had more than our share of adult mentors encouraging us to stay out of trouble and to stick to the straight and narrow.

I'd be remiss, however, if I failed to mention one person in particular who made a lasting impression in my life, as well as my family and countless other people. He exemplified what love and personal sacrifice mean in service to others. Always on call, he comforted people through their most challenging life trials and celebrated their joyous and sacred times, too. He was a man of deep faith and devotion. This person I refer to was my uncle, Father Leonard, whom our family lovingly called "Uncle."

To me, Uncle was the consummate Catholic priest: a combination of Father O'Malley from the 1944 classic Christmas movie Going My Way *(played by Bing Crosby), merged together with the soul of a humble servant of God and his people. Uncle embraced both roles beautifully. Despite the demands of the priesthood, he had a genuine, cheerful disposition that seemed to emanate from the joy that came from caring for others. Never seeking the limelight, he served as chaplain for many years at a veteran's hospital north of Chicago, comforting and administering the sacraments to the sick and dying.*

Throughout my childhood, Uncle was always a part of our lives. Besides his duties at the VA hospital, he performed baptisms, communions, weddings, and funerals for his relatives and family. He dressed as Santa Claus at Christmas, and took my parents and us kids on fishing trips to Wisconsin. He'd even bring his oversized reel-to-reel projector to our home and treat us to movies like Mary Poppins *and* The Absent-Minded Professor. *Looking back, it's hard to recall a family occasion that Uncle wasn't a part of.*

As the years passed, we kids grew up, and one by one left our parents' home to start our own lives. Of course, our parents grew older and so did Uncle. Eventually, he retired to a home for elderly priests. In time, the effects of aging took their toll and he developed Parkinson's disease and dementia, and was confined to a wheelchair. No longer was he the resilient man we once knew and admired.

One evening after work, I went to visit him. As I entered the dimly lit room, there was a motionless figure seated in a wheelchair next to a small bed. His shoulders sagged from his withered body and his head hung down. His eyes were closed, and I couldn't tell whether he was asleep or conscious.

Uneasy about disturbing the stillness of the room, I quietly sat down in the chair beside him.

Prior to Uncle, I had not experienced the heartbreak of seeing a loved one in such physical and mental decline, so I was uncertain what to expect. The man before me almost seemed unrecognizable from the Uncle I knew growing up. Once known for his immaculate appearance, he was now disheveled: his face was unshaven, clothes unkempt, and his jet-black, wavy hair had thinned and grayed. Although his hands rested on his lap, they mercilessly tremored back and forth.

Uncle slowly awoke as I softly spoke his name. I awkwardly tried to fill the empty spaces of our conversation by asking how he was doing, what the food was like, and if there was anything he needed. He mumbled in short sentences that made it difficult to tell if he understood me or if he even knew who I was. At one point, he asked me to fix a broken "contraption" underneath his wheelchair that bothered him. Although it was apparent there was no problem with the chair, I nevertheless complied, pretending to repair it.

Shortly afterward, Uncle said he was tired and wanted to sleep. He asked if I would lift him out of the wheelchair and lay him on the bed. Startled by the unexpected request, I was nervous and unsure of myself as I cradled him in my arms and slowly picked him up, careful not to lose my balance. As I held his frail body close, his arm loosely draped around my shoulder, our faces were mere inches apart. In that moment, Uncle opened his eyes just a bit and, for the first time since my visit, they were clear and seemed to look inside me. He paused momentarily, then weakly smiled and whispered, "Isn't it wonderful to help someone in need?"

Those few words stunned me as I stood there holding him, but I nevertheless got him safely into bed. Watching him now as he slept, they started to sink in. For that brief instant, the old Uncle, the man who dedicated his entire life to serving God and others, had emerged from the depths of his

> *debilitating disease to pass along a simple but profound message of love.*
>
> *A short time later, Uncle quietly passed away. He died on our wedding day, and the family that loved him so dearly celebrated his life through the Mass together.*

There is always that special relative that is legendary. We think of him or her as immortal, amazing, and a force of nature. This story is about just such a person and the writer's observations of the time when mortality trumps memories.

This amazing uncle was one who had achieved the pinnacle of Maslow's Hierarchy of Needs: that of self-actualization. He is no longer burdened by the survival, belonging, and other needs of the mere mortal. His heart, his experiences, and his wisdom allowed him to finally apply the **Platinum Rule** as a matter of course, not a result of a careful thought. There is no doubt that he knew just what to say that the other wanted to hear.

The Help of a Stranger Who Cared

*I was twenty-one. In other words, I had been out of high school for three years and counting, working fifty-five-plus hours a week, making minimal money, and at a low point in my life. It was November and time to head to the annual Thanksgiving family get-together. **Expecting the usual "What are you up to?" and "When do you plan on going to college?" questions, which I was well prepared for (yeah, no, not at all . . .), I was sitting on the couch watching the game—the usual.** I was introduced to a friend of my uncle's who happened to be there and was a complete stranger. Next thing I know, I am having this talk* *with someone I didn't know one bit, and I was completely blindsided with inspiration.*

The main thing that stuck with me was him pointing out the fact that I was capable of more. *I could survive college. I could do WELL in college. I had what it took to find SUCCESS. But, he emphasized nobody was going to hand me my dream job; nobody was going to go out and do the hard work for me.* **Long story short, I remember him reminding me a fact about life: it sucks to suck.** *There is nothing fun or good about sucking, and that is exactly what my life amounted to at that moment, and I knew it. I knew he was right . . . 110 percent.*

It changed my life completely. A complete stranger came in and opened my eyes, changed my perspective FOREVER. I grew up not caring about school. I grew up in poverty with parents who didn't get to live out their potential and get a degree or the career of their dreams.

That day, a fire was lit in me. Up until that point, I had never taken education seriously. I never seriously considered going back to school. But, there I was . . . and the vision was never so clear. That day during that discussion, I knew what I had to do. That same night, I went home and started looking/applying for schools. Now learning is my biggest priority. I see its value. I understand its power and importance. I only get one chance to be the best me. So, every day I wake up and seek opportunities to make myself better, and I honestly owe it to that one eye-opening conversation.

You never know when a mundane event—an everyday conversation—can change the course of your life. This writer's story is about just one of those events. While he gives credit to the stranger, I would say a lot of the credit goes to the author. It doesn't matter if you are sitting next to a genius if you just ignore them and focus on what you want to do or hear.

Likewise, I give credit to the stranger for NOT treating this person as a stranger, for, in fact, he was not a stranger; he was a friend of his relative. I'm sure he knew a bit about the situation that the young man was facing, AND he stepped up and said something that the young man never expected to hear: not just the truth, but the **whole** truth.

Why did the young man listen? It seems he did view the stranger as an authority—fairly high, in fact—but didn't have any kind of relationship with him. As we learned earlier, there is a direct correlation between relationship and how much one listens to another. We discovered that authority + relationship = the most impactful message.

But, most of all, the words were spoken in a way that deeply resonated and validated his own thoughts. The passion of your agreement with another's words increases exponentially when they are spoken by one whom you respect. In this case, note where he says, "He was right, 110 percent." That is a pretty high level of agreement!

So, be open to conversations that come your way, even if you weren't expecting them. As this example illustrates, any one of them could profoundly influence the course of your life.

A Surprise from My Grandmother

As I think about life-changing things that were said to me, it was my grandmother who gave me a great compliment. I spoke with her on the phone while she was in hospice. This was when I was twenty-three years old. It was a short conversation, maybe five minutes. She just talked to me about how proud she was and how she knows what great things I was going to do with my future, and that she loved me.

> *That in and of itself is not at all surprising or unusual; however, the reason it mattered was that my grandmother was a hard woman sometimes. There is no doubt she was a caring woman, but her actions were very self-centered. With age, I have come to understand that she was motivated by her own insecurities, and that is why the most innocuous action could be perceived as a slight toward her, and then all the drama that came after. So, this was very out of character, and something I still think about.*
>
> ***I am blessed that I got to experience the best side of her in her final days.*** *My biggest takeaway is that I need to spend more time telling the people who matter to me how much! I feel fortunate that I am young enough to learn this lesson while most of the people that matter are still here.*

No matter how long we know someone, we never really know the whole person. If the relationship matters, you must NEVER stop learning more about the person. In the case above, the writer experienced a side of his grandmother that he had never experienced before.

It is when we get lazy and assume that we know all there is to know about someone that we need to pay attention. Just because the person was always X, there might be a Y factor in there that will never come out if we don't give them a chance.

What I Told Others

A Grown Child's Recollection

At my fiftieth birthday party, my adult stepson, who had lived with me since he was eleven when I married his dad, gave a toast I shall never forget. He said that one of his strongest memories of the years he had lived with me, particularly in junior high and high school, was that whenever he called me at

> *work, I would* always *be available and take his call. This was before cell phones and texting, so the calls went to my office phone, and if I was not there, my secretary.*
>
> *He went on to say that it was not until he was an adult and working in a corporate environment that he understood what this meant. Regardless of what meeting I was in or to whom I was talking, if he or his sister called, I was always available to them. He went on to say that **he understood that it was a statement to them and to my work colleagues that family always, always came first for me.***
>
> *I did intentionally make this decision with children, for whom I felt responsibility trumped anything I might be doing at work. But I was touched that my son had remembered this so many years later, and that he realized the commitment it represented.*

While it seems like not much of a big deal, several stories I received focused on how the author was amazed that others received the words and/or lessons exactly as the writer had intended. Of course, why wouldn't they? The truth is that a lot of what we say to others seems to go unnoticed, if not rejected 100 percent.

The writer here was given a wonderful gift in this regard. It was recognition, many years after that fact, of something that she had said, done, and modeled years before. Not only were those actions noticed, they were revered, AND they said something about it before it would have been too late.

The Law Partner and the Cleaning Man

> *When I was in my middle thirties and had just made partner, I was trying hard to establish myself at the firm, and I got into the habit of working fairly late into the evening most every night. Typically around seven o'clock, the cleaning*

crew hired by the building would come by to clean our offices. There was a young man on the cleaning staff who would knock on my closed door almost every night and ask if I wanted the floor vacuumed and my trash emptied. Most nights I let him vacuum, and occasionally we would chit-chat for a bit when he came to my door or when he took my trash.

Over the course of several months, I got to know a little bit about him. He told me he had a day job and he was doing the cleaning work to help provide for his two sons. For me, our conversations were always just a brief and friendly distraction. He was a nice guy, and I enjoyed talking to him. He would sometimes ask me about why I was always working late, and I remember telling him that I was just doing the same thing as him—trying to provide for my kids. We never chatted for more than a few minutes, but we did speak at least a little on most nights.

After a couple of years of this, my cleaning-staff friend told me that he had accepted a promotion in his day job to an entry-level management position that would require (or allow) him to leave the cleaning job. I congratulated him, wished him well, and thought that was the end of our odd friendship.

A few weeks after he left, I got an email from him out of the blue. I assume he just found my email address on the internet, because before that we had only ever communicated in person. He thanked me for all of our talks, and he told me that I had really encouraged him to move up into management and to take on more responsibility and leadership in his other job. He thanked me for being a mentor to him, and he told me that he had looked forward to our little talks every night.

*I was honestly stunned, and deeply moved, to get his email. **For me, our conversations did not seem like mentoring or encouragement at all.** I was just trying to make friendly chit-chat with the guy who came to get my trash and vacuum my office every night. I really wasn't giving it any effort at all. There was obviously an imbalance of position in our relationship, but he didn't work for my firm,*

> *and I wasn't anything like his boss or supervisor; I was just a guy who worked in one of the many offices he cleaned.* **It truly felt fantastic to think that I somehow made a difference in his life just by being kind to him** *and spending a few minutes to talk to him. The idea that he thought of me as a mentor, when I viewed our relationship entirely differently, was really a powerful lesson to me about how we can sometimes impact people without even knowing.*

This story is the perfect example of how your words and actions mean much more to their intended audience than you can ever imagine. You just won't know which words, which people, or which times. Again, another strong argument for saying the true thing to everyone you meet.

Remember, if you are an authority who has earned respect — as this law partner was to the cleaning person — you will be heard. It does not matter whether you are intending to teach, advise, coach, or just chat; the impact will be significant to the listener. You have the opportunity with those words and that impact to do tremendous harm OR life-changing good. The happiness and satisfaction that comes from hearing that it was life-changing good makes for a happy turn of events in this story. If you really read this, you will think more about casual conversations than you ever have before . . . and THAT is a good thing.

What My Kids Valued

On Christmas Eve, I become my family's version of the real Clark Griswold. We have several traditions, but the one that I enjoy the most (because the kids tend to groan the most when I introduce it) is the annual "Family Question." One year, the question was as follows: "Which of the things your mother and I did as parents do you intend to duplicate when you have kids of your own?"

This particular wording kind of threw them. I am sure they were ready to pounce on the ever-popular topic of "Parenting I Will NEVER Duplicate with My Kids!" But, alas, this one focused on the positive . . . so it took them a bit longer.

My wife and I were somewhat taken aback when the three consensus answers were spoken.

1. We will make our kids go to Sunday school.
2. We will make our kids take piano lessons for five years.
3. We will travel outside the USA with our kids.

While we certainly remember these tactics, neither my wife nor I would have particularly put them on the top-ten list . . . let alone the top three! By the way, I can also assure that NONE of these three were something that were well-received at the time. The number of "conversations" we had about going to church, piano lessons, or the Guatemala mission trip were in the hundreds!

*We learned that everything you do and say as a parent is heard and filed away. **YOU will never know which lesson they are learning. Try to make them all good ones!***

As this story is one of mine, I wanted to make a few points that really impacted me as the writer. First, our rituals and traditions always make for fascinating revelations that help guide and inform us of the **Fundamental Questions** of "How are we doing, and what's in it for us?" status of our relationships.

Also, it is a story about how others perceive what we do and say. In this case, their words told their mother and me where we scored highest on our parenting skills. Can you imagine how it feels to hear actual compliments about specific actions you took, rules you made, words you said, and behaviors you modeled? I can tell you that it brought a deep sense of satisfaction and joy to this parent.

We never really know if we are doing things "right" or even "best," but when those you love the most tell you what you did well, that feels amazing!

The Teacher's Thank-You Note

My mom made a big point as I was growing up of modeling the act of telling people when we were happy and not just when we were mad/frustrated. We ALWAYS (growing up) would be told to do things, like ask to talk to a manager to say that a certain employee had been wonderful, or write thank-you notes to people for something nice they did (not just for gifts given)—that sort of thing.

Because it's true: people mostly just complain when they are mad, but don't take the time to give praise (and don't we know that from the teaching world!).

For the past few years, I have always had a Friday reminder scheduled on my school calendar to send a "positive parent email," just to force myself to reach out to parents at least once a week (just for one kid who jumps to mind) to say something about how a student contributed, how he/she has grown as a student, something nice he/she did for another student, etc.

The response from parents is amazing. (I'll paste in one sample below. Nothing life-changing, but I'm just trying to notice positives and not only things to criticize. And, sometimes it's hard! It takes only a minute to do this, yet it creates a lot of positive vibes.)

Note to Parents

I just wanted to send you a quick email to let you know how much I am appreciating Anthony and his contributions to my history class. His work and thinking are a step above most of my other students, and there is so much depth to his knowledge. Today, we did a group editing activity, and he was SO helpful to the other students in his group. It was like having another teacher in the room.

I know teachers tend to write home only when something isn't going well in the classroom, but I thought I'd send you a happy Friday note with some good news. :)

Enjoy your weekend, and thanks for all you've done to raise such a neat, smart kid!

Note to Teacher

Thank you so much for the nice email. It's always good to hear when things are going well. He has truly been enjoying school this year, and even talks about it with us from time to time. ;)

And, of course, we would be remiss if we didn't thank you and all his great teachers. It has been an extraordinary time for him, and we are always impressed with the things he comes home having learned.

On top of that, though, you all manage to create an environment that helps to bring out the good side of middle schoolers, which is no easy task.

Thanks again for the note!

The above story is a fascinating example of the long-term, maybe even latent, impact of what others say to you. In this case, it was a somewhat annoying requirement of her mother. The requirement seems like it was well-intentioned, but like the piano lessons in "What My Kids Valued" earlier, maybe not their most favorite way to pass the time. It's tough as a young person to talk to strangers, much less compliment them.

But, the amazing part is that to this very day, the writer, now a teacher, continues the habit that her mother instilled into her many years ago. What an impact! A lesson learned as a child, when practiced as an adult, becomes a gift—a gift that continues to give when we see the chain of compliments from mother to daughter and from daughter to student's parents, and from the student's parents back to the teacher. That creates a powerful chain of respect, kindness, and love passed along.

The Security Guard

I was around thirty years old or so. I worked for a sizable local restaurant chain, and the company had grown fast during the late seventies and early eighties. I was in charge of auditing the restaurants and security (i.e. catching the thieves in the restaurants). We had grown so fast that we had our operations spread out into several buildings around the Kansas City area. Corporate decided to build a building on the Country Club Plaza. All of our current sites had building management and security. The new location would be our responsibility.

After about two weeks in the building, items started to disappear. Small items at first, but one day the president demanded to see me and said his laptop and several expensive items had "disappeared," and he wanted to know what I was going to do about it! Since I hadn't been involved in the design and building phase, I was a little shocked and upset. I just inherited a very large project with little time or planning availability.

I contacted our security company for the restaurants and they came out immediately. But, it would take several weeks to put a system in place to handle this building. I also contacted a guard-service company, but they couldn't start until the next day. Guess who stayed all night at the building the first night? Yep, yours truly!

The next day at around 6:00 p.m., the guard service came with the team that would be working until 7:00 a.m. the next day. One young man looked like he was terrified! The uniform he had on was "one size fits all," and he would have to take three big steps before the pants would start moving. I was really beat, and I was about to leave, when I turned to him and asked if he was okay. He didn't know what to say at first. Then he opened up, and he told me that his wife was very pregnant, and he was told he could not call home (before cell phones) and could not leave the building until the next morning. He didn't know what to do. About this same time his supervisor came up and asked if there was a problem. I replied no, but that I wanted (and I pointed at the young father-to-be) the team to use the phone at that front desk to be able to call me during the night if the team had any questions or if there were any issues. The supervisor said of course.

The next morning, the young man thanked me and said his wife was so grateful. A couple of weeks went by, and he asked me if we could talk. He said something was troubling him. I asked him what was wrong, and he said he figured I was about his age, yet he was a starting security guard and I was (in his view) a very successful person. He asked me how I did it. Wow, what a question! I didn't view myself that way at all. I didn't know how to answer or what to say. I told him to grab a coffee and come up to my office.

We sat and talked, and I told him how I got the job. I wasn't the smartest or the most experienced. I was the one that volunteered to do the jobs that others didn't want to do. I was the one that wouldn't ask anyone to do a job that I wouldn't do. I stayed late and came in early. *I wanted to learn, and I told my supervisors that. Then I asked him what he wanted to do, and he said he didn't know. He said that most of the other security guards took naps and* *didn't care while they worked. It was just a paycheck. He wanted more. I said that was easy; just do what I did and give it time.*

Several years went by, and my wife and our three-year-old came down to the building to meet me for lunch. About the same time, our front-desk receptionist called me and said I had visitors who just came in. I asked who and didn't recognize the name, and then she told me the man had what looked like his entire family with him. I was very puzzled.

When I came around the corner, the man in a suit handed a baby to the woman with him while he said something in Spanish, and her eyes contacted mine. A large smile was on her face and that of the man. He came over and took my hand and wouldn't give it back. I know I had the look of "What is going on here?"

He said his name several times and it meant nothing to me. Then his wife, holding the baby and another child around four or so, came up to me, and he introduced us all. I was still lost. He said he was that security guard from several years ago! He said he took my advice and worked very hard for the company. He had been made a supervisor and then put in charge of a region! He and his family had just bought their first home and they were on the way to the bank closing, and he wanted to stop by and say it wouldn't have happened without me. I introduced my wife and daughter to them, and I know I was in shock.

How did my simple act of doing the right thing have such an impact? *To this day, I keep reminding myself that the effort of taking time to help someone can have giant dividends of which you may never know about.*

This story is quite similar to the lawyer and the cleaning-crew member. In fact, I have heard stories like this several times. This one is slightly different because the advice and words offered were solicited by the guard asking the writer a question.

The writer took the time to be specific with his reply. No platitudes, no confusing answer, no impossible-sounding scenarios. What he tells the guard is straightforward and doable. Those words and that advice from someone who the young guard perceived as "respected and an authority" were internalized. In fact, they were acted upon, and the results show the power of those words.

The Last Row of the Plane

It had been over nine months since my life had changed in a material way. I had been let go from the company I founded by the acquiring company. As monumental as that seemed at the time, the passage of time had significantly helped put this episode in my rearview mirror. In fact, this story begins with a joyful event of love and celebration.

I had just completed a very exciting business transaction, and to celebrate, I decided to surprise my wife with a trip to Chicago. But, as my friends say, I never just "do" anything. I'm kind of known for my creativity, and this would be no different. I wanted to totally surprise my wife with this trip. I felt I owed her a very special surprise, because I have to admit that I had not been the most joyful and fun partner for the past few months. It was time to change all that!

I made all the arrangements: plane, hotel, babysitter. I even had the courage to pack her bag without her knowing it. In fact, as part of my espionage, I took a stealthy photo of her makeup that was out on an average moment so that I might know what to pack for her.

So, the morning came, and she thought we were going out for breakfast, but little did she know we were on our way to the airport. I had done it! And finally, with the recent business success and the happiness of "the old me" pulling this surprise off, I felt like myself again. At that moment, I finally found the opportunity to tell my wife how much she meant to me and to thank her for providing me strength during those challenging times.

Then, we got to the airport. We cleared security and looked for a place to sit down in the crowded lounge area. I excused myself to get by the extended legs of a man who was working on his laptop. He said how sorry he was, and suddenly called out my name and said, "Hey! How are you doing, buddy?" The person speaking those words was the person who was given my old job shortly after I left the company. Talk about a buzzkill! At that moment I felt deflated, and all those thoughts from the past several months came flooding back. My wife instantly noticed the change in me.

I regret that there was nothing I could say other than small chit-chat. I have often wished that I could have shown him how well I had recovered, how much I wished him success, and how I did not hold him at all accountable for what happened. I know that would have made us both feel much better. But . . . I just could not find the words (or the strength).

We finally left the lounge (thank goodness) and boarded our flight. Of course, in keeping with the day, my wife and I took our assigned seats on the very last row of the plane with the wall on our back and seats that do not recline. Why not? On top of that, seated across from us was a young husband, wife, and three small kids! What a flight this would be.

In the next moment, all that changed when the young man leaned across to say that he recognized me from a photo he had seen years ago on our company website, and asked if I was indeed the owner that he remembered. I was taken aback and said yes, I was, but had no idea why he was asking that.

His face lit up, as though he was seeing a superstar/hero of his. He said, "I am so thrilled to be able to meet you in

person and tell you how much you have meant to our lives."
He said he had been studying accounting in college and was
hating it. He happened on our website and said to himself,
This is what I want to do. *That led him to change his*
major, delay his graduation, but land a job at a firm doing
exactly what he loved to do. He said that I (a perfect stranger)
was the catalyst, and wanted to thank me in person.

I was mostly in shock and thanked him. I asked him why
he was traveling. He said he was on his way to Florida after
attending the funeral of his father, who had passed away
unexpectedly the prior week. He said that meeting me had put
a wonderful sunlight onto a very sad time, and felt it was fate.

Funny, he had no idea what our chance encounter and his
words had meant to me. I glanced at my wife, who had heard
all this transpire, and saw she was wiping away tears of joy.
Whether you call this fate, or God's will, or just an amazing
coincidence, I can honestly say that this stranger gave me
exactly the gift that I needed at exactly the right time, and I
will never forget this moment for the rest of my life!

This was a story I never anticipated. I am sharing it here because
I really am not sure where to place it. Sometimes things happen to
us that we cannot at all see coming. It is only in looking back on
them that they seem to make sense.

This is one of those stories. It is the "trifecta" of stories: there is
an element of regret, an element of redemption, and a very
important element of restoration . . . *both* giving and receiving. See
if you can identify each element as the story unfolds.

Lessons from Stories of Restoration

The reason that I call these stories "restoration" is because they
nearly always represent a turning point, a fork in the road, and a
decision to change that is brought on by someone in their lives.

As you can see, these stories are different because in most situations:

- They are not planned, but come about often through the regular course of life.
- They are often not in response to any obvious and current situation, but become relevant to the listener either now or some relevant time in the future.
- It is not uncommon that the messages are delivered by someone who is not close—or sometimes even unknown—to either party in the conversation.

What is true and typical is that the right person came along at the right time with the right message. They could articulate that message in such a way that the listener was able to process it. The words are usually spoken by someone who is either respected and loved, or is seen as an authority, but again, this might not even be apparent at the time to the speaker.

Our lesson is to learn that we must find ways to be open to great advice, great words, and great teachings all the time, because we never know who or what or when those pearls will be given to us. Also, we need to know that what we say and what we do is listened to and observed by many people, not just the intended parties. We all have the opportunity to spread the *words that matter* all the time.

The challenge is that we are human and that it is not easy. None of us are perfect, and sometimes we say exactly the wrong thing at the wrong time. Again, we might not even know that either, but it happens. No advice in a book or from others can save us from saying the wrong thing . . . or even from saying nothing. It is hoped that by sharing these stories of amazing restorations, we can learn more about how and why to try our best.

Chapter 7
Now What?

Maybe these stories have inspired you to take action. Maybe you saw yourself or your relationship in one of them. Maybe you saw an idea for how to finally act on your feelings with the words that matter.

As with so many things in our lives, the decision to actually say something is the most important decision, and should be the first decision. If you have made that decision, then it just comes down to identifying the *who, what, when, where, how,* and the all-important *why.*

Let's take a look at each of these.

Who

Who is able to speak this truth?

This is never easy, and it is the rare individual who can behave with this level of transparency, empathy, and feeling 24/7 with everyone. My younger sister is blessed to be one of those people, as you can tell from the following way that she answered my questions and penned her story.

These questions you posed are very difficult for me, because I believe I am someone who always *lets people know how important they are to me. As I think about my personal experiences, here is what I have found.*

- *I think family and those closest to us are the ones we try to honestly speak to the most. But even that takes care, because if it's too much, it sounds disingenuous, and if it's not enough, it is hurtful.*
- *But, I believe fear of rejection and people's own pride and embarrassment keep them from honesty.*
- *I believe I have always told the people who are important in my life how important they are. Some people don't care, and they*

maintain a distance anyway. But, I believe that is their own issue, not my lack of honesty.

- *I have had numerous people close to me tell me how wise I am. They have said such things as, even though I have lost my singing voice (my sister had the singing voice of an angel until thyroid surgery changed that forever), God has given me a voice to speak truths and love to people. That has had a huge impact on me, especially when it comes from people who are not family or in your immediate sphere.*
- *Nothing makes me more joyful than knowing something I said had a positive impact on someone. I truly subscribe to the notion of "Leave people better than when you found them."*
- *And her final thought on the subject sums it up incredibly well: "I am an incredibly honest person, so if honesty has ever cost me anything, then it really wasn't mine to begin with."*

My goal with this book is to reach out to the rest of us who have challenges with this type of communication, but also have a desire to have great relationships. My point is, choose your *who* carefully and start slowly. If you can be open, honest, and transparent with a mere handful of relationships in your life, you can count yourself as a fortunate person.

Consider the following quote that resonates with many.

"Being honest may not get you a lot of friends, but it'll always get you the right ones."

—John Lennon

To whom do we reach out?

I must admit here that I was originally going to recommend sitting in silence to think about the following questions that will help you determine who you need to tell.

- Who are the most important people in my family?
- Who are the most important people to me in the rest of my personal life?

- Who are the most important people to me in my business/professional life?
- Which ones of them *know* that they are important to me?
- What would they say if I asked them what they meant to me?
- Which ones might have a different answer to that than I might?

Those are the ones to think about telling first!

However, as I began to really read and hear the many stories related earlier, I realized that these questions were positioned 100 percent backward. Read the revised list below:

- Who are the people in my family *who need to hear* these words the most?
- Who are the people in the rest of my personal life *that need to hear* these words the most?
- Who are the people in my business/professional life *who need to hear* these words the most?
- Which of them *know* that they are important to me?
- What would they say if I asked them what they meant to me?
- Which ones might have a different answer to that than I might?

You can see the difference here. The second set of questions better illustrates the **Platinum Rule** of saying unto others what *they* would have you say unto *them*. It's not about you and who is important to you, nor is it about me and who is important to me. It's about the people in the various spheres of our lives and whether we've been honest with them. Have we been forthright in our words and actions with them?

In addition to the revised set of questions above, I might also add, "Am I encouraging them? How have I encouraged them?" for those I am closest to, and "Am I a fount or a drain?" for the people I may not be as close to.

You see, it really doesn't matter who we each think is important. It matters that we get better at speaking the truth in love to all who cross our paths on life's journey. Recall the times someone said something uplifting or promising to you (or reread some of the **Stories of Restoration**). Then, ask yourself if the person who said them did so because you were important to them, or because it was important to them to speak the truth in love to someone who crossed their path.

If anyone, anywhere is in your *who*, and you are living true to your core values which provides the *why*, then the *when* is *always*.

What

The next task is to think about what we want to say. This is challenging, to be sure, because as mentioned earlier, one of our greatest fears is rejection of what we say. Again, my best advice is to not overthink it. As they say in the communications world, do not over-message. Saying *one* important thing that you believe *they* want to hear is the task, and that is certainly enough if your intent is pure.

When

This is also a very tall and strong barrier for many of us. It seems weird to meet someone, get to know them, develop a relationship over a long (or even short) period of time, and suddenly, right in the middle of it, STOP and interject such a strong sentiment. We all wish there were a recognized and universally adopted "Time for Deep Thoughts and Words" when everyone knew it was time to say these things. But, there is no such thing now. *You* have to create that for yourself.

There used to be. When I was a child, I have vivid memories of the retirement party that was thrown for both my grandmother and my grandfather. As soon as they turned sixty-five, their retirement was announced, and their employers held a gala evening that my child-sized memories captured as fancy, dressed up, a ton of speeches, serious food, gifts, and a big table up front with my Pinky and Pop (what we called them) and a bunch of other grown-ups.

Following a nice dinner, it was now time for those in their life to stand up, take the microphone, and expound on the virtues of my dear grandparents. Not sure how sincere they were (I was only about nine years old), but at least there was a time and a place. In fact, everyone seemed to enjoy themselves, and stress was not apparent to me. But then again, I was a kid!

Absent such a fortuitous event for your relations, you unfortunately have to be the one to decide when to do this. There is no correct answer, but depending on your anxiety level, perhaps you can use some of the ideas that I will share with you in Chapter 9 of this book. Some of them are pretty creative and work quite well.

But, what matters most is that you have to wait for AND watch for the right moment. What is the state of mind of the listener? If they are preoccupied with work stress or just had the world's worst day, they will likely neither hear your words, nor receive the intention behind them. In fact, you risk being MISHEARD, which has more potential to do more damage than we think.

Where and How

For this type of communication, the *where* is completely up to you. Just make it a place where you both are comfortable (so, likely not in front a bunch of people if it is a private thought) and a place conducive to good conversation (probably not a stadium or movie theater). The location of the place can say a lot about the intent, so it wouldn't hurt to give it a bit of thought.

If it is to tell a valued associate at work how much you respect them and appreciate them, why not take them to a place you have heard them mention that they love? If you don't know one, perhaps you are not listening enough. Again, if you reflect on the **Platinum Rule**, you will be able to transport yourself into the listener, and the perfect spot will come to you.

As for the *how*, just give it a bit of thought and begin a conversation of value (as opposed to just daily chit-chat). Tell them there is something you would like to say to them, and then say it. Remember to be direct, specific, and come from a place where you already feel you understand what *they* want to hear.

An example might be, "I have never taken the time to tell you what you mean to me as a friend. You always seem to wonder if you are *enough* to others or to me. Well, you are more than enough. In fact, whether you know it or not, you are my *best* friend. And to me, that means that when there is something in my life—good or bad—that I need to share, I want to share it with you, because YOU get me! I just want to thank you for that and pray that we will always be this close."

There is no doubt that the speaker here had a great communication with the listener.

1. **The Platinum Rule:** The listener had wondered if she was enough, and the speaker told her YES with certainty. That certainly follows the rule of "Say unto others what they would have you say unto them."

2. **Our Fundamental Questions:** The speaker did an excellent job of answering the questions of "How am I doing with you?" (*"Whether you know it or not, you are my best friend."*) and "What does that mean for me?" (*"I just want to thank you for that and pray that we will always be this close."*)

While we can always strive for more in our communications, the real *how* should always begin with successful communication of #1 and #2 above.

One last word about the *where* and *how*: not all situations call for a face-to-face conversation. While generally the most impactful, sometimes it is just not possible due to distance or too uncomfortable for a number of reasons. Several of the stories discussed telephone or written conversations. All other advice remains the same, just the method of delivery has changed . . . and that's okay!

Why

Last but not least, remind yourself of *why* you want to have this conversation. Only you know the true reason, and only the most selfless reason will make it worthwhile.

A former colleague and dear friend of mine, when asked *why* and the reason for its importance, answered as follows:

Over the past few years, I've adopted the practice of speaking truth, beauty, and kindness into people's lives. What does that mean?

I discovered a deep personal need in myself to understand how I've made a difference in the lives of those around me. It's true that these words are rarely spoken. And, while I'm rarely gifted with that truth, I figured that the world would be a better place if I offered out what I so deeply craved: something true; something beautiful; something kind.

So, when I see something beautiful and true and kind in another, I speak that truth into their lives. Because in the long run, and in a world where we've become so disconnected, we need to remember we all live in the shelter of each other, and are each of us contributing to the quality of the energy we're bringing to the people in our lives.

I believe this to be a beautiful and articulate way to express one's *why*. I only wish I could do it so well.

Remember always to give without thought of receiving anything in return.

Remember that you really want them to know exactly how you feel, no matter how they receive it. And most of all, remember that *not* saying anything will do nothing to improve the relationship, and is bound to lead to unnecessary failure and subsequent guilt in the future.

"You can't blame someone for walking away if you didn't do anything to make them stay."

—Unknown

Chapter 8
Rituals, Traditions, and Activities to Try

In the course of researching this book, one of the things I heard most often about why words that matter are so hard to give is that it is an awkward subject to bring up just in the middle of life. People said it would be easier if we had a designated "time to gush," where it was a safe place and space to say these things.

I am blessed to have had the opportunity to "borrow" some great ideas to use for this for both family and nonfamily relationships. Likewise, I have had the opportunity to create some interesting new ideas to try.

For family times, I am already called the "Clark Griswold" of the family because of how many times I work to create these opportunities. Corny, yes, but I'm pretty sure if I ever stopped, I would hear "So . . . whatever happened to that lame question thing you always made us do?"

Likewise, at home, at work, or around friends, it is rituals, traditions, and our unique activities that create amazing culture and relational bonds. This can be between two people (*"My best friend and I always are in the stand together on the first day of deer season . . ."*) or an entire company (*"The Halloween party we do each year is amazing! No one does it quite like this . . ."*).

All relationships greatly value and, in fact, *need* the cultural connection of these rituals and traditions. If your family or team of friends do not have any, start one. If they have them, never let them end. Step into a leadership role if you have to, but keep them alive, for these are the times and places where the equity in the "relationship bank" is filled up. These are the places where it is safe and okay to have "designated relationship talks." These are also the moments that create the memories *and* the conversations that matter.

Care Cards

This is a tradition that began with our youth pastor. They were used on several church mission trips we all attended during the kids' junior and senior high school years. We recently adapted this idea to our family vacations.

I don't know about your family, but the early years of family vacations were a breeze. The school system and the calendar basically dictated the times to go: spring break, Christmas vacation, and summer break. Funny—when the kids are out of school and start spreading out geographically, that all falls apart. One of the more difficult things to reignite is the annual family vacation.

We have finally found our rhythm, and it includes eleven of us, as of this writing (grandkids continue to appear on a fairly regular basis!). For now, the care-card ritual just includes the adults, but will soon include the grandkids. Last year, we did the following.

On the first evening of the vacation, Clark Griswold (yours truly) hands out blank 3" x 5" cards to each of the adults. Every adult receives a blank card for each of the other adults. The mission is for each person to write the answer to the designated question on a separate card for each of the other family members. On the final night after dinner (with some adult beverages in hand), we assemble and read each card out loud to each individual in front of the whole group.

For example, last year the designated question was: *"Name three things you MOST admire about each member of the family."*

What is so amazing is how seriously everyone takes this. During the vacation week, I would be walking by the patio window and peer out to see my daughter-in-law, pen in hand, working on both her tan and the 3" x 5" cards! In the wee hours of the morning, I would walk by my youngest son's room and see him lying in bed, headphones on . . . writing the 3" x 5" cards.

The question changes every time. A list of great questions would include replacing "things you most admire" with words like "personality traits you most enjoy," "personality traits you most respect," "What are the adventures or experiences you would like to have with X?"

The idea is to make us take the time to think about the relationships we have one on one with each individual of the family. To reflect on what you *most* want to say to compliment them, and to write that down and actually say it. I don't have to tell you that the "reading of the cards" on the final night is a time that is permanently seared into the memories of each of us under "Times I Felt Really Great about My Family (and My Life)."

Thanksgiving Dinner

This is a very easy starting place for families, friends, or even small groups. It is such an easy one to execute because it comes at a time when we are told it is "Thanks Giving" day. All we need is a time and a place and someone to get the ball rolling.

My suggestion is to use this as an opportunity to sit, relax, and chat *after* the meal is done. There are many ways to do this, but one that I like is to look to the person to your left and say, "Nancy, I am most thankful for knowing you because . . ." and just fill in the blank. You continue around the table until you get to the end, and then you reverse and go back the other way. This way, you must at least "give thanks" to two people at the table.

To avoid people "figuring it out" and plotting their seating arrangement, the leader will, of course, designate a completely different batting order each year. This provides fun, diversity, and keeps us guessing. It is spontaneity that works best here. Often times, the conversation continues after the round robins are done, and that is a good thing!

Christmas Eve

Everyone always wants to open gifts on Christmas Eve. It leads to endless debates and awful compromises. Who wants to open socks or pajamas on Christmas Eve and then call it a day? But, conversely, who wants to wake up Christmas morning only to realize you already opened everything?

So, consider starting the "Twelve *Ways* of Christmas" present-giving event. Everyone buys—or preferably makes—a Christmas card for everyone they will be with on Christmas Eve. Each person then writes down the twelve things that each person in the room has given to them this past year. I know it sounds hard, but it is amazing how many things you can come up with when you pause and think about it.

The beauty of this is the sheer inundation that each receiver will feel with positive reinforcement and unconditional love. When you consider the hours you put into buying the perfect gift, why not trade a few of those for the honor of giving the perfect words that are specific, real, honest, and happy? I know we won't remember what item we received last year, but I know we will remember the things that were said for a lifetime.

New Year's Eve

Okay, so you are on to me and are seeing the trend and the theme. I'm not being lazy, but have learned from experience that it is easier to insert a tradition into an existing event than to create a tradition AND an event.

This one works well for the office (at a year-end meeting, for example), for friends (just prior to watching bowl games), and of course family. It is a take on the New Year's resolution. However, this has a great chance of actually happening since it is being shared with friends and/or family who matter and who care.

Each person involved will make a New Year's resolution to each of the other participants. The resolution will be to recognize, reinforce, and elevate the one amazing personal gift that each of the other participants has. In other words, you first must name it (i.e. "Bill is my role model for living a healthy lifestyle."). Then, you resolve to continue to recognize that gift in him/her, and to call it out when you see the trait and continue to make them feel excited about it throughout the year.

Birthdays

The birthday is an obvious time of celebration in one's life. Unfortunately, as we grow older it goes from a world-class childhood mega-fete to a "maybe no one will notice" nonevent. I think this is because the celebration at the beginning was about getting older and growing up. The celebration in the later years is about being old and getting older.

Let's change that AND work on our relationships at the same time. We often use the phrase "You are not getting older, you are getting better!" So, let's put our words where our mouth is. Again, make or buy the perfect card that actually says those words (there are usually dozens of them on the racks). But, this time you have to write exactly *what* it is that has made that person *better* this past year.

It must be specific; it must be about your relationship; be emotional; and it must have some depth (eating twelve doughnuts in one setting will not do it). It will touch the person in a very special way. It will tell them where they succeeded in your relationship. It will NOT talk about where they came up short. It will spell out EXACTLY how *they* rocked your world this past year.

Like all declarations of this variety, the one who delivers the message will gain two-fold. First, they will have spent some time thinking about that person and the relationship prior to writing or saying anything. Secondly, after that reflection, they will have the joy of seeing the gift received so positively by the recipient. Better than a mass-produced greeting card, this one is personal. But, the true gift is in speaking love and truth to the receiver.

Office "Tellabration"

This is an opportunity to tell others great news that was inspired by the "Thank You, Bill" story, which was the final story in the **Stories of Redemption** section. This was where we sat the celebrant down and went around the room, each saying what he/she meant to them.

It is well known that offices have an abundance of celebrations. There are innumerable birthdays, wedding showers, baby showers, retirements, promotions, etc., etc. As I reflect back on the hundreds of events like this, what I see and feel in my mind's eye is sheet cake, punch, and highly uncomfortable officemates standing around like middle school students at the beginning of their first school dance. Then someone comes in, says blah, blah, blah, the person blushes and opens the gift, and then everyone wanders back to their cubicles.

I'm sure they were nicer than that, but I'm pretty sure there might be a better way. What if the office party was planned in the same way as my peer-group goodbye event?

Whoever is being celebrated sits or stands in the center of the room, and each one of us says something very specific and very nice about that person. To avoid putting anyone on the spot, there should be a designated person who solicits and gathers these comments ahead of time. Of course, not everyone will have something to say; that is not the point. The point is to make sure that there are enough kind words and that the person feels that those in the room really know them and care about them. While it is nice to have a party thrown by your officemates, it is even better to hear nice things from those you respect, admire, and/or love.

Make a Date: "Remember to Remember"

My son-in-law is a very thoughtful young man. He is one of the best I know at taking the time and effort to say "thank you" to those around him. I asked my daughter about this, and she said it is from a discipline that he adheres to stringently. Every week, there is a time on his calendar set aside for "thank you." It can be a letter, email, text, or phone call, but every week he does at least one. In that time, he covers the *who, what, when, how,* and *why* of a thank-you, and then he executes it.

As the recipient of several of those notes of appreciation, I can say with certainty that they really pay off. I can't imagine my father-in-law writing about me as a role model. That shows you how powerful this event is in maintaining the relationship. While the thanks are not necessarily life-changing events, they nonetheless add up and keep the relationship vibrant and alive.

Others have said that it is the enforced "taking the time" to think about our relationships that really makes the difference. If we intend to do it, we never do it. If we schedule it, we do! So, I am suggesting that we modify this task as follows.

Once per week, we mark a half hour on our calendar titled "Remember to Remember." During this time, you must stop and think about relationships. Go over the questions I sent to my network in Chapter 6 that helped inspire the stories that followed. Even if you do not act, you will then think about these people that mean (or meant) so much to you. Many of the writers of the Chapter 6 stories wrote that the act of stopping and thinking about these relationships was as valuable as writing about them or even acting on them.

However, I'm pretty certain that if we regularly take the time to think about these wonderful parts of our lives, we will eventually do something about it. We will act, and it will be life-changing for each of us.

Letters to Each Other

This technique is often used in marriage counseling and in addiction scenarios. They are used to allow open communication *after* that communication has gotten into some trouble. Just like preventative health-care, what about a preventative exercise to keep the communication going before trouble begins?

These letters are mostly for those that are very close to you. Also, they are meant to be the result of pretty serious self-reflection on the relationship and some meaningful written words. However, this letter will not be given or sent; it is to be read aloud together with the individual, and they will read theirs back to you.

The format of the letter is to answer in a very specific way our **Fundamental Questions** we all have from Chapter 2:

"How am I doing with you?"
"What does that mean for me?"

Of course, there are better ways to word these questions that will likely yield a better result, but they should attempt to get those important questions answered. For example, the instructions could be as follows: *"Write a letter to (name) that tells them why they are so important in your life. Be specific and use examples. Then say why that matters to you and what that means to YOU!"*

And, as always, remember the **Platinum Rule**: "Say unto others what THEY would have you say unto them."

All-Star Performance Review

This is the replacement (or supplement to, if you aren't ready to exercise the demon yet) for the dreaded annual performance review. What is unique about this one is that there is no "BUT." There is no "room for improvement." There is only honest, sincere, and specific praise. BOTH sides have to write this. The review must focus on the last year, and must relate specific examples that actually happened and that both of you know about.

After it tells each other what is remarkable and outstanding about the person being reviewed, it must also give a vision of what it all means for them. For example, the form could look like this:

How are we doing?
1. In my opinion, what is the most valuable thing you did for the company this year?
2. What is the most valuable thing you did for me this year?
3. What are you significantly better at this year than prior years?
4. Who have you really gone out of your way to help this year?
5. Where did you really "take one for the team" this year?

What's it mean for me?
There are so many strengths, there are many options for what happens next. Let me be your coach and mentor. Tell

me where YOU would like to be on next year's strengths, and I'll promise to help you get there.

BESTimonial

This is my favorite idea—and one that I have never tried and never even heard of. However, I will be so bold as to suggest that from the day you read about it, you should make it your personal mission to plan and execute one in the next year. I'm certain that once you do one, you will never get enough.

As I mentioned earlier in the book, there was once a tradition of the retirement party back when people spent their entire careers with the same organization. That was the time that office workers, bosses, friends, neighbors, and families were invited to a formal, fancy shindig. The entire purpose was to celebrate the person retiring with speeches, awards, gifts, and maybe even a gold watch.

Those days are over. From observing the millennials I know, it seems like there is a lot of job changing, especially in the early stages of their careers. That does not lead to twenty-five-year retirement parties, nor to the gold-watch tokens of yesteryear's careers.

So, I am advocating the beginning of a new family (or friend) tradition. It is the BESTimonial: a party where it is ALL about the honoree, and nothing is said but amazing things about that person. It is a "This Is Your Life" program for every one of us. It is, most importantly, given *before* eulogies and funerals, when the person is still alive and able to participate and listen.

I think it is the regret of doing a great job on my dad's speech, but without him there to hear it, that led me to this mission. Why not? Can you imagine how you will make a loved one feel when they hear what wonderful things others have to say? Of course, they will be embarrassed. Of course, they will feign anger at you for this. BUT, believe me, it will certainly immediately become one of the top-five memories of their lives.

And, as we have learned, do you know who will receive the greatest joy from this? You know who will reap the greatest gifts from this event? It will be YOU, the one who put it together! That is the amazing part. This statement is so true that I am dumb-founded that this tradition is not well under way yet.

I know there are a lot of details to work out and logistics, but the most important thing I want you to take away from this idea is the *why*!

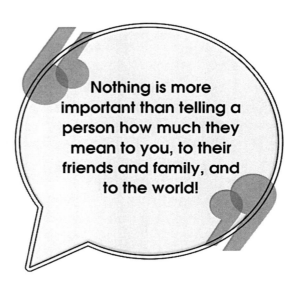

> Nothing is more important than telling a person how much they mean to you, to their friends and family, and to the world!

Giving a loved one the gift of being able to hear about their legacy in real time while they are still living will certainly be one of the greatest gifts we could ever give. After all, I have never seen an angry person seated in the Kennedy Center box receiving their Medal of Freedom, nor do I see a lonely and unfilled person receiving their Hall of Fame award. Why not all of us? Why not now?

Epilogue

After reading and thinking about this subject for some time and rereading the stories shared earlier, there are a few conclusions that I feel would be appropriate to make.

While all communication is difficult, it seems that saying unconditional **words that matter** is even more of a challenge. There are many reasons for this, but the fact remains that one of the more pervasive reasons for regret in our lives is our inability to say just how we feel about those in our lives.

There seems to be a value in taking some time to reflect on the questions relating to our relationships that contemplate:

- The times *we haven't told* those we value how we really feel
- The times *we have told* those we value how we really feel
- The times when *others tell us* how they really feel about us

In fact, many of the stories relate the writer's gratitude for being given the opportunity to rethink the situations and the outcomes of the important relationships in their lives. Here are some comments from the writers that reflect this value:

"I spent time thinking about these three questions, and my biggest takeaway is that I need to spend more time telling the people who matter to me how much! I feel fortunate that I am young enough to learn this lesson while most of the people that matter are still here."

"I think your book is very timely and right on point. If we develop the ability to articulate our ideas and feelings, we will experience less anger and frustration with our peers, spouses, and coworkers."

"Thank you for helping remind me to pause and remember someone dear to me."

"I think 'love' should be in the title. I really do. I don't think you are going to wordsmith anything that conveys the meaning like 'love' would, and it really is love that is at the center of what you are talking about (in my opinion)."

"Is it our fear of our love being rejected, our hesitation to admit that we feel love for other people, some kind of weird power dynamic, fear of exposing ourselves through our emotions . . . I really don't know. Maybe a combination of those things, maybe something else entirely. I will continue to think on this."

"Communication has been part of my thoughts almost on a daily basis as it has continued to emerge in my daily life on how many people there are on earth, each with their own identities, having some slightly different interpretation of messages. Trying to help people with your experience and intelligence in many ways is highly dependent on peoples' capability or need at any given time to RECEIVE the information. You will have the content. The challenge, as with most things, is one's interest in getting information on topics. I am excited to see you push this book into execution!"

"Just reading the questions brought a tear to my eye. This is a highly difficult task you've requested and places the author of these particular stories into a truly introspective mindset. It would seem, however, that the exercise will prove cathartic."

Some further observations also became apparent following the reading of the stories.

When it comes to regret, a surprising number of the stories indicated that there is still time to do something about it. In one case ("The Cool-Kids Table"), the writer actually *did* do something, and the results were life-altering for both parties. Perhaps by thinking about what got us into this situation, there might be the realization that whatever it was will *not* get us out of here. If we desire a change and there is still time, why not try?

The reason this is so important is profoundly exhibited in the **Stories of Redemption**. One of the most significant similarities of these stories is how much peace and reward the redemption brought to the one who DID tell the other. While it is nice to hear nice things, it is apparently even more awesome to say them. I remembered an important lesson from an experienced copywriter who I worked with early in my career. He said:

"When people are standing at the card rack reading and rereading all the cards for just the right sentiment, it is not just how appropriate the message is for the receiver of the cards. No, sir. It is more about you imagining what the receiver will be thinking about you when they are reading that card!"

He went on to explain that it is, in fact, the way that a gift makes the giver feel that perpetuates gift giving. While we all want to make our loved ones feel joy and happiness, we care even more about how they feel about us, remembering Maslow's Hierarchy and our two **Fundamental Questions:** "How am I doing with you?" and "What does that mean for me?"

We also learned a lot about the power of words in the **Stories of Restoration**, the stories where others spoke to us. These moments move us in significant ways. The very course of our lives is changed because of what others, especially those who truly matter, say to us. While not all are 100-percent positive, the motive and the relationship are such that their words sink in and move us to change in a positive way. It is remarkable how many of these words have lasted for years, decades, or even a lifetime.

It is equally amazing how potent the words are that *we* give to others. We are seen as authority figures by many. We are respected and/or loved by many—often more than we know. This brings me finally to our responsibility. We need to realize how much words do matter, and also realize that we do not always know which of our words delivered at which time to which person matter to them. We need to continuously remind ourselves of this.

About five years ago, my then twenty-five-year-old youngest son told me something that I will never forget. He and I were sitting late one night on the back porch, talking about how much better our relationship is now that he is older. We hypothesized several reasons that might be true, but never really concluded anything other than time and maturity . . . and the fact he was NOT a teenager anymore!

I remember telling him how much it frustrated Mom and me that he never listened to us, no matter how many times we told him things. But, we were now so proud that he was beginning to exhibit the values and characteristics that we were talking about. What he said was profoundly simple: "Dad, I heard *everything* you and Mom said, *every time*. It was up to me to decide what to do about them and when."

Wow, I have never felt so mixed in my life—selfishly thrilled because he really had heard what we said, and that all that effort did not go to waste, and stunned by how we never really knew that he had heard those words.

Finally, while what we say to our children is important, what we say to EVERYONE is also important. The first instinct I had upon reading the stories in this book is to personally apologize to everyone in my life who I have hurt, offended, demotivated, or made sad with my words. Whether that impact was intended or not, remembered or not, meant or not, is not the point. I hope someday they read these words and know that I am truly sorry. No ifs, ands, or buts, just *I'm sorry.*

The point is that all of us must take care with our words to use them to bring happiness, confidence, joy, and belonging to those around us. Emerging along with the trend of daily mindfulness is the following quote, which proves as an extension to our central theme "words matter." It's called the Three Gates of Speech:

"Before you speak, let your words pass through three gates.
At the first gate, ask yourself, 'Is it true?'

At the second gate ask, 'Is it necessary?'
At the third gate ask, 'Is it kind?'"

—Rumi

The premise encourages us to reactively guard our words before we speak them, but I posit that these criteria can and should be the cornerstone for proactive sharing of our truths with all those who cross our paths, especially those we love.

Those we love, those we work with, those we know, and even those we don't all matter in the end. I don't want any of us to spend our lives regretting the mistaken things we said, nor those we never said at all. I want us to learn a new habit of bringing positive words into the lives of those that matter to us.

Together, let's change from:

Discussion Guide and Exercises

Many of the amazing Vistage speakers that teach our peer advisory boards utilize handouts that help us continue to generate greater value from their topic after they have left. I have always appreciated that, because it is difficult to condense what they have said into actions.

It is my hope that after reading this book, you will be motivated to work on how you can help them really tell what needs to be said to grow their relationships, and how to work with family, friends, colleagues, or teams to do the same.

To that end, here are a few questions or exercises to help guide you. Good luck!

1. Susan Scott said, "Our work, our relationships, and our lives succeed or fail one conversation at a time."
    a. Give an example of a time that just ONE successful or failed conversation materially changed a relationship of yours.

2. In Chapter 1, we discussed how the effect of someone's words is in direct proportion to their level of love and/or respect for that person, and their position of authority and/or commitment over them.
    a. Do you agree with that? Why?
    b. Give an example of a person in your life that fits each of the categories below:
        *   Someone for whom you have great love and respect, but who has no direct authority or commitment to you or the subject

- Someone for whom you have little love or respect, but who has authority or commitment to you or the subject
- Someone for whom you love and/or respect a great deal, AND is a significant authority and commitment to you and to the subject

   c. Give us an example of something that was said or not said to you by one or more of them. Share with us how much or how little it impacted you.

3. Think about your most important relationships at home, in the office, or among your friends. Do you know where you stand with them using the above criteria? Take a moment to fill in this chart *about you* from *their point of view.* So, if you believe your boss would view me as someone they love and respect, put an X in that box. If you do not believe they do, leave it blank.

When complete, review what is missing in each relationship that will hinder you from being a positive force for good in each person's life. Discuss with team the best way to improve the situation.

Name and Relationship	I Believe That They Love and Respect Me	I Believe That They View Me as an Authority and/or a Committed Member of the Team

4. Have you ever said any of these things to someone who means a great deal to you?

- "Since you never said anything, I assumed that you didn't care!"
- "Well, I'm no mind-reader!"
- "You never say that to me anymore."

   a. Write down at least three other things you could say to that same person that would likely yield a different and more positive outcome.

5. Discuss the real differences between the **Golden Rule of Communicating** and the **Platinum Rule of Communicating**.

   a. The **Golden Rule of Communicating**: *"Say unto others what you would have them say unto you."*

   b. The **Platinum Rule of Communicating**: *"Say unto others what they would have you say unto them."*

6. Give an example of a situation where you used the **Golden Rule** and should have used the **Platinum Rule**. Do you feel the outcome would have been different?

7. Discuss your thoughts on the suggestion that the only two things people really need to know are:

   a. How am I doing with you?

   b. What does that mean for me?

8. Write down your current top-five relationships (include family, friends, coworkers, etc.). Do *you* know the answers to the following two questions for each of those relationships? Are the answers based on factual information or assumption?

   a. How am I doing with you?

   b. What does that mean for me?

9. Who would you most like to give you the definitive answers to the two **Fundamental Questions**? What specific impact(s) would that have on you?

10. Have you ever decided not to compliment someone? Explain the relationship and situation. Why did you stop?

11. If you had a job performance with your best associate that had no "but," what would you say? Write it out and try once to see what happens. What is the hardest part? Writing it, or giving it to them?

12. Review the story types at the beginning of Chapter 6 and repeated below, and come up with three examples. Name the person and the situation.
    a. One, where it is too late to change the outcome
    b. One, where there is time to change the outcome, but you are not sure you can or want to
    c. One, where there is time to change the outcome and you are committed to do it

---

I would like you to share a personal story about one or more of the following questions about a relationship(s) that you have had. The categories and questions are as follows:

1. Stories of Regret

Tell me about a time where you believe a relationship was significantly impacted because you didn't really tell the other person how much they meant to you.

a. What was the nature of the relationship (business, family, romantic, friend, etc.)?

b. Tell me about how it ended (resigned, passed away, walked out, faded out, etc.).

c. Tell me what you now think you should have said.

d. *Tell me why you did not say it (fear or rejection, no urgency, assumed they knew, etc.). Did you ever come close? What stopped you?*

2. Stories of Redemption

Tell me about an experience where you did take the time to say exactly what was on your mind and feel that action impacted the relationship.

a. *What was the nature of the relationship (business, family, romantic, friend, etc.)?*
b. *Tell me what you did say and how you said it (location, timing, mode of communication, etc.).*
c. *Tell me what happened and how it felt to do this.*
d. *How did you manage to tell them how you felt? Was it scary?*

3. Stories of Restoration

What others told you: *Tell me about a time that someone told YOU something that REALLY made a positive difference to you. What was one of the most wonderful/meaningful/significant compliments (or positive/loving criticism/suggestion) you ever received? (When I think back, the number of those is very limited, but they really made an impact on me . . . even after many years!)*

a. *Who was it that gave you the compliment (coach, boss, family member, teacher, friend, etc.)?*
b. *What were the circumstances of the time you were told (when, where, how old were you, in person or not)?*
c. *What did they say?*
d. *Why did it matter?*

What you told others: *Tell me about a time that someone told you that YOU told them something that REALLY made a positive difference to them.*

a. *Who was it that told you about what you said?*
b. *What difference did it make in their life?*
c. *Do you even recall the time/place or saying it?*

13. Take those three names and review Chapter 5. How do you do it?
    a. How can you take the "nonfixable" situation and somehow gain peace?
    b. How can you decide whether to fix a situation?
    c. How can you make it happen when you decide you want to?

14. Finally, create your own story based on the three story types at the beginning of Chapter 6. Share them with someone not involved in the situation, and discuss them in depth.

15. Who would you give an apology to if you could? Why? Why have you not done it yet? Can you make it unconditional? Why not? What can you do about it now? What do you want to do about it now? What will you do about it now?

16. Which of the rituals, traditions, and activities from Chapter 9 will you commit to doing? Why? Which one do you want to do but are not yet ready for? Why? Who can help you?

17. Do you have your own example or idea of a new Chapter 9 activity? Share it with your team.

18. What do you want people to say about you at your **BESTimonial**? Be specific about who says it and what they say. Why do you wish that? What are you doing today to make sure it happens the way you want?

About the Author

Jeff Hutsell is a highly successful executive coach and an award-winning chair for Vistage Worldwide, the world's largest chief-executive organization.

Prior to becoming a coach, he was an accomplished executive in the social-expression category of consumer products, working for such companies as Hallmark, The Franklin Mint, and the Enesco Group, where he ultimately became the president and CEO. Additionally, he was the founder and CEO of Levels of Discovery, makers of premium children's furniture, until he sold the company in 2013.

Hutsell earned his undergraduate degree at the University of Kansas and received his MBA from the Harvard Graduate School of Business.

He currently resides in Overland Park, Kansas, with his wife, Sara. He is the proud father of three wonderful children and four grandchildren (so far!).